Best Climbs
Denver and Boulder

Sara Born gliding up *Calypso* on Wind Tower in Eldorado Canyon near Boulder. PHOTO BY MATTHEW KELLEY

Best Climbs
Denver and Boulder

Over 200 of the Best Routes in the Area

STEWART M. GREEN

GUILFORD, CONNECTICUT
HELENA, MONTANA
AN IMPRINT OF GLOBE PEQUOT PRESS

Dedicated to the great Denver and Boulder climbers who established these Best Climbs for our enjoyment, including Dale Johnson, Ray Northcutt, Layton Kor, Pat Ament, Larry Dalke, Jim Erickson, Steve Wunsch, Alan Nelson, and Ken Trout. Thanks for your vision, boldness, and hard work!

To buy books in quantity for corporate use
or incentives, call **(800) 962-0973**
or e-mail **premiums@GlobePequot.com.**

FALCONGUIDES®

Copyright © 2011 by Morris Book Publishing, LLC

FalconGuides is an imprint of Globe Pequot Press.

Falcon, FalconGuides, and Outfit Your Mind are registered trademarks of Morris Book Publishing, LLC.

All interior photos by Stewart M. Green unless otherwise noted.

Maps and topos by Sue Murray © Morris Book Publishing, LLC
Text design: Sheryl P. Kober

Library of Congress Cataloging-in-Publication Data
Green, Stewart M.
  Best climbs Denver and Boulder / Stewart M. Green
    p. cm.
  Includes index.
  ISBN 978-0-7627-6116-6
  1. Mountaineering—Colorado—Denver—Guidebooks. 2. Mountaineering—Colorado—Boulder—Guidebooks. 3. Colorado—Guidebooks. I. Title.
  GV199.42.C6G73 2011
  796.52'209788—dc22   2010034453

Printed in China

10 9 8 7 6 5 4 3 2 1

WARNING

Climbing is a sport where you may be seriously injured or die. Read this before you use this book.

This guidebook is a compilation of unverified information gathered from many different climbers. The author cannot ensure the accuracy of any of the information in this book, including the topos and route descriptions, the difficulty ratings, and the protection ratings. These may be incorrect or misleading, as ratings of climbing difficulty and danger are always subjective and depend on the physical characteristics (for example, height), experience, technical ability, confidence, and physical fitness of the climber who supplied the rating. Additionally, climbers who achieve first ascents sometimes underrate the difficulty or danger of the climbing route. Therefore, be warned that you must exercise your own judgment on where a climbing route goes, its difficulty, and your ability to safely protect yourself from the risks of rock climbing. Examples of some of these risks are: falling due to technical difficulty or due to natural hazards such as holds breaking, falling rock, climbing equipment dropped by other climbers, hazards of weather and lightning, your own equipment failure, and failure or absence of fixed protection.

You should not depend on any information gleaned from this book for your personal safety; your safety depends on your own good judgment, based on experience and a realistic assessment of your climbing ability. If you have any doubt as to your ability to safely climb a route described in this book, do not attempt it.

The following are some ways to make your use of this book safer:

1. Consultation: You should consult with other climbers about the difficulty and danger of a particular climb prior to attempting it. Most local climbers are glad to give advice on routes in their area; we suggest that you contact locals to confirm ratings and safety of particular routes and to obtain first-hand information about a route chosen from this book.

2. Instruction: Most climbing areas have local climbing instructors and guides available. We recommend that you engage an instructor or guide to learn safety techniques and to become familiar with the routes and hazards of the areas described in this book. Even after you are proficient in climbing safely, occasional use of a guide is a safe way to raise your climbing standard and learn advanced techniques.

3. Fixed Protection: Some of the routes in this book may use bolts and pitons that are permanently placed in the rock. Because of variances in the manner of placement, weathering, metal fatigue, the quality of the metal used, and many other factors, these fixed protection pieces should always be considered suspect and should always be backed up by equipment that you place yourself. Never depend on a single piece of fixed protection for your safety, because you never can tell whether it will hold weight. In some cases, fixed protection may have been removed or is now missing. However, climbers should not always add new pieces of protection unless existing protection is faulty. Existing protection can be tested by an experienced climber and its strength determined. Climbers are strongly encouraged not to add bolts and drilled pitons to a route. They need to climb the route in the style of the first ascent party (or better) or choose a route within their ability—a route to which they do not have to add additional fixed anchors.

Be aware of the following specific potential hazards that could arise in using this book:

1. Incorrect Descriptions of Routes: If you climb a route and you have a doubt as to where it goes, you should not continue unless you are sure that you can go that way safely. Route descriptions and topos in this book could be inaccurate or misleading.

2. Incorrect Difficulty Rating: A route might be more difficult than the rating indicates. Do not be lulled into a false sense of security by the difficulty rating.

3. Incorrect Protection Rating: If you climb a route and you are unable to arrange adequate protection from the risk of falling through the use of fixed pitons or bolts and by placing your own protection devices, do not assume that there is adequate protection available higher just because the route

Denver/Boulder Overview

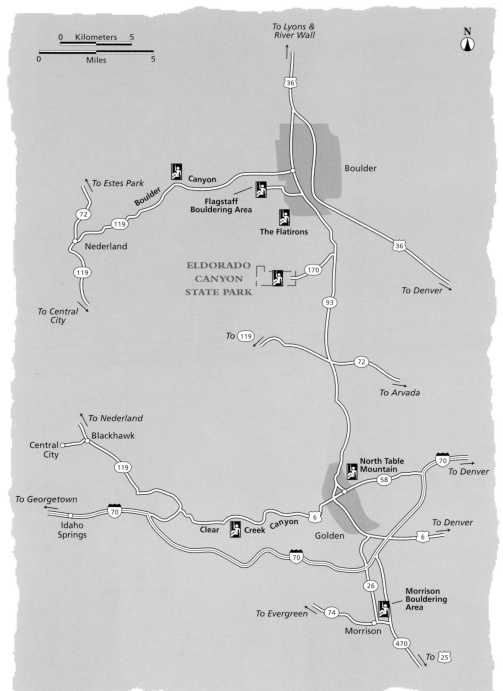

0 — Kilometers — 5
0 — Miles — 5

N

To Lyons & River Wall

36

Boulder

Canyon

Boulder

Flagstaff Bouldering Area

The Flatirons

170

ELDORADO CANYON STATE PARK

36

To Denver

93

To 119

72

To Arvada

To Estes Park

72

119

Nederland

119

To Central City

To Nederland

Blackhawk

Central City

119

70

To Georgetown

Idaho Springs

Clear Creek Canyon

North Table Mountain

58

70

To Denver

6

Golden

6

To Denver

70

26

Morrison Bouldering Area

To Evergreen

74

Morrison

470

To 25

Contents

Introduction

The Front Range skyline above Denver and Boulder offers some of Colorado's best and most varied climbing adventures, from long, easy scrambles up the tilted Flatiron faces to short, fierce testpieces in Clear Creek Canyon. In between are lots of moderate sport climbs at Golden Cliffs, multi-pitch traditional-style gear routes up soaring sandstone walls at Eldorado Canyon, a multitude of sport and trad lines on compact granite crags in Boulder Canyon, two handfuls of stellar sport routes on Colorado's best little cliff—the River Wall—and Flagstaff Mountain, Colorado's historic bouldering area.

Climbing Seasons

Climbing is possible year-round along the Front Range west of Boulder and Denver, with the shoulder seasons of spring and autumn offering the best weather. Spring, from March through May, brings variable weather. Expect warm, dry days sandwiched by cool, windy days with occasional rain or snow. Summer days are usually hot, with highs creeping into the 90s. Look for shady cliffs during the heat of the day. Also watch for thunderstorms, which quickly build over the mountains like clockwork in the early afternoon. Plan your climbs accordingly by going in the morning, being prepared for rain, and retreating when lightning plays on the ridges. Autumn is the ideal season for your best climbs, with warm, sunny days and cool nights. Precipitation is usually light and short-lived. Winter brings wild and variable weather. While many days are frigid and snowy, stretches of sunny high-pressure days are also found. Look for south-facing cliffs to maximize warmth and daylight.

Land Management and Closures

All of the crags are on public land, and include Boulder Open Space, Roosevelt National Forest, Eldorado Canyon State Park, Access Fund land, and Jefferson County Open Space. The boundaries between the different tracts of public land as well as adjoining private property are often blurred. Use your best judgment to avoid trespassing and controversy. Also check for restrictions before placing bolts and fixed gear, which is illegal without prior permission on Boulder Open Space property and at Eldorado Canyon State Park.

Some cliffs are seasonally closed for raptor nesting. These areas include parts of Boulder Canyon, the Flatirons, and Eldorado Canyon. Most closures occur from February 1 until July 31. Check with the land management agency for complete closure information. Closures are usually posted at trailheads and

Ian Spencer-Green climbing *Mr. Squirrel Places a Nut* at the Golden Cliffs, high above Denver.

sometimes at the base of popular climbs. Cliffs in this book that are usually closed include the Third Flatiron, The Matron, and parts of Redgarden Wall.

Climbing Rack

While gear suggestions are included in many of the route descriptions, what you carry on your climbing rack is up to you. Look at your proposed route and decide what you need to safely protect yourself when you climb.

If it's a sport climb, count the number of bolts and add a couple more for the anchors. For traditional routes, bring a standard rack that includes sets of RPs, Stoppers, and cams to 3 inches. Also bring eight to twelve quickdraws and three to five slings with extra carabiners. Some climbs might require an off-width piece, and others, particularly in Eldorado Canyon, are often protected with Aliens or other small Tri-cam units.

A 165-foot (50-meter) rope works great for almost all the routes in this book. If you use a 200-foot (60-meter) or longer rope, you can often run pitches together. Just remember to make sure your rope is long enough if you're lowering someone off a sport route, so you don't drop her.

Climbing Dangers and Safety

Rock climbing is dangerous. That's a fact. The perils of climbing, however, are usually overstated. The risks we take are the ones we choose to take. Everything we do as climbers, including placing gear, setting anchors, tying into the rope, and belaying, is to mitigate the dire effects of gravity and to minimize the danger of climbing. It's up to you to be safe when you're climbing. Be safety conscious and use the buddy system to double-check your partner and yourself.

Redundancy is key to your personal safety. Always back up every important piece of gear with another and use more than one anchor at belay and rappel stations. Your life depends on it. Beginner climbers are most vulnerable to accidents. If you're inexperienced, hire a guide or take lessons. Always use sound judgment when climbing, and respect the danger. Don't get on climbs beyond your ability and experience. Remember that most accidents happen because of climber error.

Objective dangers, as at most climbing areas, abound at the Denver and Boulder cliffs. Watch out for loose rock as you climb or if another party is climbing above. Loose flakes and boulders are common, particularly after freeze-thaw cycles in winter. Wear a helmet to mitigate head injuries when climbing and belaying. Use any fixed gear with caution. Some climbs still have old pitons and bolts, and it's hard to determine how secure they actually are. Always back up fixed gear with your own. Poison ivy is found along many cliff bases. Keep an eye out for shiny leaves and small white berries. Rattlesnakes are found at the low-elevation cliffs, particularly at Clear Creek Canyon and Golden Cliffs. Weather can be fickle. Thunderstorms move in quickly, so be prepared to bail off your route if necessary. Rain can come down fast and heavy. Watch for lightning on high points at Eldorado Canyon and the Flatirons.

Use the following ten tips to stay safe when you're out climbing on the cliffs around Denver and Boulder:

- Always check your harness.
- Always check knots.
- Always wear a helmet.
- Always check the rope and belay device.
- Always use a long rope.
- Always pay attention.
- Always bring enough gear.
- Always lead with the rope over your leg.
- Always properly clip the rope into carabiners.
- Always use safe and redundant anchors.

To learn more about climbing, including basic skills like creating anchor systems, placing gear, jamming cracks, rappelling, belaying, and tying knots, buy my comprehensive instructional book *Knack Rock Climbing,* co-authored with Ian Spencer-Green, from FalconGuides.

Be prepared for emergency climbing situations by bringing the Ten Essentials:

Navigation
Sun Protection
Insulation
Illumination
First-Aid Supplies
Fire
Repair Kit and Tools
Nutrition
Hydration
Emergency Shelter

Map Legend

Symbol	Description	Symbol	Description
70	Interstate	○	Town
25	US Highway	�’	City
74	State Highway	🧗	Climbing Area
170	County Road	⬭	Crag/Boulder
= = = = =	Gravel Road	∿	Cliff Edge
▬ ▬ ▬ ▬	Unimproved Road	▲	Mountain Peak
··············	Trail	🅿	Parking
∿	Waterway	🚻	Restroom
⬭	Lake/Reservoir	⬠	Building
≋	Falls	▲	Camping
⌐ ─ ─ ─ ┐	National Forest/ State Park Boundary	•—•	Gate

Topo Legend

○	Natural gear belay stance
x	Single piece of fixed protection (bolt or piton)
xx	Fixed belay station

Boulder Area

Boulder, a university town nestled below the Front Range, is simply Colorado's best destination climbing area. The Flatirons, immense sandstone slabs pasted on Green and South Boulder Mountains, loom above Boulder and form its distinctive mountain backdrop. Hundreds of climbing routes lace the sandstone slabs and their steep west faces, giving climbers lots of routes in a wilderness setting. Eldorado Canyon, protected as a Colorado state park, is an awesome gash carved by South Boulder Creek as it races from the Continental Divide to the plains. Eldo's angular sandstone cliffs have long been considered one of America's best rock climbing arenas, with climbers from around the world coming to test their skill and nerve on its vertical landscape.

Directly west of downtown Boulder lies Boulder Canyon, a rough-and-tumble gorge lined with granite crags that offer excellent crack and face climbs. The sandstone boulders and spiny ridges on Flagstaff Mountain compose one of Colorado's oldest and most historic bouldering areas. Legendary climbers like John Gill, Pat Ament, Layton Kor, and Jim Halloway all made first ascents on Flagstaff's sharp blocks. The River Wall, a small granite cliff tucked into a hidden canyon, is called "the best little crag in Colorado" for its classic bolt-protected face climbs above the North St. Vrain River.

Come to Boulder and ascend its classic best climbs, hang out at its great climbing shops, microbreweries, and coffee shops, and enjoy its laid-back athletic ambience—and you might never leave.

Boulder Area

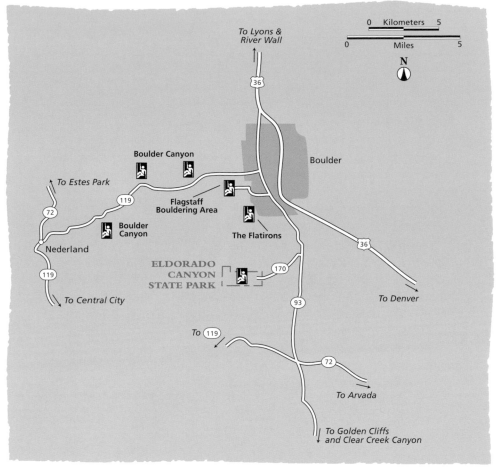

To Lyons &
River Wall

0   Kilometers   5

0   Miles   5

N

36

Boulder

Boulder Canyon

Flagstaff
Bouldering Area

To Estes Park

119

72

Boulder
Canyon

The Flatirons

Nederland

36

119

ELDORADO
CANYON
STATE PARK

170

To Central City

93

To Denver

To 119

72

To Arvada

To Golden Cliffs
and Clear Creek Canyon

1.

Boulder Canyon

Boulder Canyon is a spectacular 14-mile-long canyon west of Boulder. The canyon walls, lined with numerous granite crags, domes, and buttresses, form an impressive climbing area with more than 1,500 routes up to four pitches long on over one hundred named crags. The canyon crags offer lots of bolted sport climbs as well as traditional gear routes with varied climbing that includes delicate slab moves, thuggish cracks, and overhanging gymnastic faces. Boulder Canyon has lots of great climbs for climbers of all abilities, making it one of Colorado's most popular climbing areas.

Boulder Canyon's cliffs are easily reached from CO 119, which follows Boulder Creek up the canyon to Nederland. Numerous pullouts for parking are found along the road. Be careful crossing the busy highway. Some cliffs are reached by Tyrolean traverses above rushing Boulder Creek. Again, use caution during high water runoff in spring and early summer. Some cliffs are closed for raptor nesting from February 1 to July 31, although none of the ones included here have closures.

Getting there: Boulder Canyon is easily accessed from downtown Boulder. Drive west on Pearl Street, Canyon Boulevard, or Arapahoe Avenue. Canyon Boulevard, which is CO 119, is best. If you're approaching from Denver on US 36, follow the highway north from Baseline Road, where it turns into 28th Street. Turn left on Canyon Boulevard just past Arapahoe and drive west. Follow Canyon Boulevard west to the canyon mouth. All mileages to the cliffs and parking areas begin from the bridge at the junction of Canyon Boulevard and Arapahoe Avenue just west of the Boulder city limits.

THE DOME

The Dome is simply one of Boulder's finest crags. The south-facing granite cliff offers lots of classic gear routes, is easy to access, and lies a scant ten minutes from downtown Boulder. It's crowded on weekends. Communication can be a problem when the creek is running high.

Finding the crag: Drive west from downtown Boulder on Canyon Boulevard (CO 119). From the bridge at the junction of Canyon and Arapahoe Avenue at Boulder Canyon's mouth, drive 0.5 mile and park at a large pullout on the north side of the highway just past a road cut.

Boulder Canyon

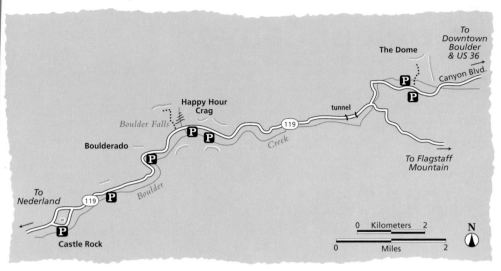

Walk along a rock buttress and cross Boulder Creek on a bridge. Go right on a trail until you're below the cliff. Scramble up a climber trail that leads to The Dome's base. Hiking time is ten minutes.

Descent: Descend from the summit by downclimbing either the east or west side of the crag.

1. East Slab (5.5) Fun classic route. Begin below an open slab. **Pitch 1:** Climb a short corner, then move up left to the slab. Cruise the slab, following a couple cracks, to an overlap. Pull over and climb up right to a cliff-top belay. An alternative belay is below the roof.

2. Cozyhang (5.7) Start just right of the cliff's toe. **Pitch 1:** Climb a

slab to a triple roof. Pull past the top one (5.7) and climb up left to a cozy belay below a big roof. **Pitch 2:** Traverse under the roof (5.6), then climb a slot to a ledge. **Pitch 3:** Climb an easy corner to a roof. Reach over (5.7) and climb an easy slab to the summit. A great variation heads directly up a leaning crack (5.10a) to the summit slab.

3. The Owl (5.7) Great jamming. Begin below an easy slab. **Pitch 1:** Scramble up the slab, then move up left. Work up right below a roof, turn a corner, and jam a hand crack (5.7) to a ledge. **Pitch 2:** Same as *Cozyhang's* third pitch.

4. The Umph Slot (5.8 to 5.10) The name says it all. It's a narrow slot

The Dome

through a roof. Difficulty depends on your body size. Skinny is better than chubby. **Pitch 1:** Climb easy rock to the slot base and belay. **Pitch 2:** Umph and squeeze up the awkward slot. Belay on a ledge above. **Pitch 3:** Climb a corner up right, pull over a roof (5.10a), and smear an easy slab to the top.

5. Super Squeeze (5.10d) Classic toughie. **Pitch 1:** Climb *Prelude to King Kong* or climb to the base of *The Umph Slot* and move up left to a belay below a huge A-shaped roof. **Pitch 2:** Jam an angling hand and finger crack (5.10d) over the roof to an awkward exit. Climb easier slabby rock up right to a summit belay.

6. Prelude to King Kong (5.9) to *Gorilla's Delight* (5.9+) Two good pitches that demand respect. **Pitch 1:** Jam a thin crack up a left-facing corner left of a black streak to a belay. **Pitch 2:** Jam a hand crack up an over-hanging corner (5.9+), then step right to another crack. Jam a couple moves and smear out right on a steep slab. Friction up it to the top.

7. Left Edge (5.7) Start at the left edge. Climb an easy slab to some roofs. Work over them and follow a curving corner to a big roof. Keep left and follow a dihedral to the cliff top.

Brian Shelton easing up low-angle terrain on *East Slab* (5.5), The Dome, Boulder Canyon.

HAPPY HOUR CRAG

Happy Hour Crag is one of Boulder Canyon's most popular climbing venues, especially on evenings after locals get off work. The south-facing cliff offers lots of routes, mostly of moderate grades. Come early or on weekdays to have the crag to yourself. If the parking lot is full, it's busy up there.

Happy Hour is popular for toproping since the crag's summit is easily accessed by foot by hiking up a gully on the left side of the cliff. If you're toproping, bring slings and webbing up to 30 feet long to rig anchors from trees and gear. Use extreme caution when setting up topropes. Don't knock rocks off and make sure you're tied in on the cliff edge. Serious accidents have occurred on the cliff top. Bring a rack with sets of Stoppers, TCUs, and cams to 4 inches if you plan to lead. No sport routes are at Happy Hour, and only a few of the routes have bolt anchors.

Finding the crag: From the bridge at the junction of Canyon Boulevard and Arapahoe Avenue at Boulder Canyon's mouth, drive west up CO 119 for 6.8 miles and park in a pullout on the left (south) side of the highway. Happy Hour Crag is high on the slope directly north of you. Cross the highway and hike up a steep trail to the west end of the cliff base. Hiking time is ten to fifteen minutes.

Descent: Descend from the top by scrambling down a steep gully on the west side of the cliff.

Happy Hour Crag has been the scene of many toproping accidents and a few fatalities. Use extreme caution on the cliff top when setting up your anchors. Make sure that you're tied into the end of your rope and that it's firmly anchored if you're creating a toprope anchor at the cliff edge.

1. Left Side (5.5) Crack system on the far left. Good beginner lead with lots of gear. Climb past a triangular block to a hand crack.

2. I, Robot (5.7) Start right of a tree. Climb a shallow right-facing dihedral, then finish up a crack.

3. Are We Not Men (5.7) Start just right of *I, Robot*. Work up a right-facing corner and easily pull over a roof. Continue up a crack to the top.

4. Twofers (5.8) Quality climbing. Start at the base of a groove. Climb a right-facing corner on the left to a short dihedral to a roof. Make exciting moves left around the roof and climb easier rock to the summit.

5. Twofers Bypass (5.8) Variation to *Twofers*. Climb to the dihedral below the roof, then launch up right along an angling crack system.

Happy Hour Crag

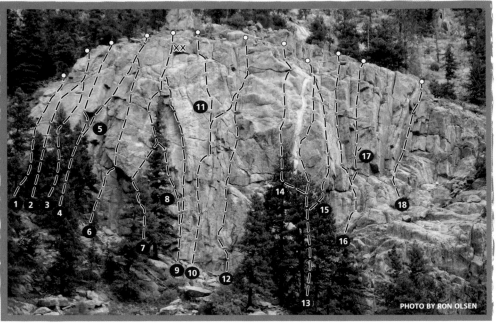

PHOTO BY RON OLSEN

6. The Big Spit (5.9) Begin below the left side of a big roof. Climb a corner to the roof, turn it on the left, and jam a good crack.

7. Rush Hour (5.12a) Start below the right side of the roof. Climb a corner to a hanging flake. Traverse up left and make strenuous moves over the roof (5.12a). Follow easier cracks to the top.

8. Last Call (5.9+) Sustained, physical, and good. Begin in the crack system right of *Rush Hour*. Climb cracks to the base of a left-facing corner. Work up left past some roofs to a tricky traverse left. Finish up *Rush Hour*'s cracks.

9. Dementia (5.10a) Best on the cliff. Start up the next crack right of *Last Call* and climb to a V-shaped left-facing corner. Jam the finger crack up the tight corner. Above, finish up cracks to a 2-bolt anchor.

10. Malign (5.7) Varied moves and good pro. Climb a broken right-angling corner system, keeping right of a painted peace sign and a steep face to a final open book.

11. Thrill of the Chaise (aka Cheers) (5.10a) Climb *Malign* to the peace sign, then launch directly up a steep face past a couple bolts and nut placements to a 2-bolt anchor below the top.

12. Nightcap (5.9) Good climb with a short crux. Climb broken cracks to an open dihedral. Stem and jam up the dihedral past a bulge to more corners to a crux upper bulge. Finish up a nice crack in a corner.

13. Grins (5.8) Excellent jamming. Start at a rock spike at the cliff's low point. Climb 50 feet to a hanging tooth. Jam a good crack up the face right of a vertical white pegmatite band to the summit.

14. Last Laugh (5.11a) The face left of *Grins*. Climb *Grins* to the top of the hanging tooth, step left to a bolt, and climb directly up past two more bolts to a high crux and anchors on a ledge. 3 bolts to 2-bolt anchor.

15. Teetotaler (5.11a) Climb *Grins* to the tooth or broken terrain to the right. Climb to the base of a hanging arête. Work up the arête with heel hooks and palms past four bolts. Finish at *Grins*'s 2-bolt anchor or the cliff top.

16. Hands Off (5.7) Short but fun. Scramble up easy rock to the base of a dihedral. Stem and layback up the dihedral to the top.

17. The Great Race (5.9+) A short toughie. Scramble to the base of the crack and corner right of *Hands Off*. A tricky start leads to easier climbing.

18. Cruel Shoes (5.9) Stem up the short dihedral on the far right side of the face.

THE BOULDERADO

The Boulderado, a southwest-facing cliff, rises above the north side of the highway. The cliff, named for a landmark Boulder hotel, is deservedly popular with its perfect granite and sunny exposure. On nice days, particularly on weekends, ropes usually hang from almost every route. It's perfect for beginning leaders and for toproping. A couple routes have bolt anchors, while others require long slings to rig toprope anchors from trees and gear. The four routes on the steep right side are much harder than those on the main face.

Finding the crag: From the bridge at the junction of Canyon Boulevard and Arapahoe Avenue on the west side of Boulder, drive west up CO 119 for 8.6 miles. Park on the left (south) side of the highway in a spacious pullout. Cross the busy highway and hike up a climber trail to the cliff base. Hiking time is five minutes.

Descent: To descend from the cliff top, scramble down the left side to the base.

1. Jam It (5.8) Start at the cliff's left side below a big roof. Climb easy rock to a crack in the right side of the roof. Hand jams up the crack lead to a scrambling slab finish.

The Boulderado

2. Ho Hum (5.4) Edge up a slab to a pine tree on a ledge. Step left and climb a right-facing corner. Finish up left to the top.

3. Idle Hands (5.6) Excellent. Climb a slab to a bulge to a crack system. Face climb up a headwall to an easier finish.

4. Mons (5.5) Smear up a fun slab, then jam a short crack. Work up broken cracks above to the cliff top.

5. Fistula (5.4) Another slab start leads to an easy fist crack.

6. Qs (5.9+) Good climbing on the left side of the lower right face. Face climb left of an edge. 6 bolts to 2-bolt anchor.

Around the corner to the right of *Qs* are three hard routes: *Jazz on the Mezzanine* (5.12b), *Hell in a Bucket* (5.12d), and *Suite 11* (5.11c).

CASTLE ROCK

Castle Rock, one of the Boulder's most famous crags, towers above the highway's south shoulder. A gravel road swings around the south side of the cliff, giving easy access to the climbs. Almost sixty routes and variations ascend Castle Rock, ranging from 5.0 to 5.14. Expect good crack climbing on the moderate trad lines. Bring a standard Boulder rack with sets of Stoppers, TCUs, and cams to 4 inches.

Finding the crag: The rock, towering above CO 119, is 11.9 miles

west of Boulder. A gravel road turns south at the crag's northwest corner and swings around its south face. Park below the impressive south face. The longest approach is thirty seconds.

Descent: Descend from the summit by downclimbing the north face to a pine tree with a rappel chain. Rappel and scramble down to a path that leads west to the road. Use caution, particularly in winter or after rainstorms, when descending. Many routes also have rappel anchors.

1. Skunk Crack (5.9+) Locate two cracks. *Skunk* is the left one. Bouldering moves lead to a shallow chimney to a crack on the right. Climb easier rock to a 2-bolt anchor.

2. Comeback Crack (5.10b) Jam a finger crack to a bulge, then climb an unprotected prow (5.7 R). Finish at a 2-bolt anchor.

3. Curving Crack (5.9) Layback or jam a corner crack. Stem and layback a left-curving corner to a roof. Above, climb a crack to a 2-bolt anchor. **Descent:** Rappel.

4. Bailey's Overhang (5.8) Follows a right-facing corner. **Pitch 1:** Jam a fist crack to a ramp. Climb the ramp to a wide crack. Awkward moves lead past the overhanging crux, then jam a crack in a right-facing corner to a belay from a horn to the left. Rappel 105 feet from a cable around a block to the ground or do **Pitch 2:** Climb easier cracks and corners to the top.

5. The Final Exam (5.11a) No topo. Classic bouldering problem. Climb a 20-foot bulge with fingertip laybacks. Above the problem, climb slabs to the *Pass/Fail Option* (5.11a) roof, traverse right to *Coffin Crack,* or downclimb slabs to the left.

6. Coffin Crack (5.10b) No topo. Strenuous off-width crack. **Pitch 1:** Wrestle up an off-width crack to a belay above the slot. **Pitch 2:** Above, jam a hand crack over a roof (5.10) and climb to the top. **Descent:** Walk off or after pitch 1, rappel from anchors 15 feet right from the belay.

7. The By Gully (5.9+) No topo. Immediately right of *Coffin Crack*. **Pitch 1:** Climb an insecure crack, then thrutch up an off-width crack and a couple slots. Scoot left and belay atop *Coffin Crack*. **Pitch 2:** Climb up and over a roof and continue up.

> After leading the first ascent of *The By Gully* in 1964, Royal Robbins said, "By golly, it went."

8. Cussin' Crack (5.7) Good moderate. Start in an obvious cave/cleft. **Pitch 1:** Climb a chimney up the cleft (5.5) or the slab right of it (5.8) to a trough. After 65 feet, exit left and climb up left to a belay stance below a corner. **Pitch 2:** Climb cracks into a V-shaped corner—Cussin' Crack. Work up the corner (5.7) to a long corner (5.6) to a good belay ledge. **Pitch 3:** Scramble up easy rock to the top.

9. Jackson's Wall (5.6) Popular and fun classic. Begin at the left side in a cave. **Pitch 1:** Long pitch. Climb the cleft up right past chockstones, then up a diagonal trough to a face. Go right and climb to a ledge with a 2-bolt anchor. **Pitch 2:** Stem up left and climb a headwall (5.6) to a ledge. Climb up right to the summit. **Descent:** Scramble down the north side, trending left to a tree with a rappel chain.

10. Tongo (5.11a R) Begin around the corner from *Jackson's Wall*. **Pitch 1:** Follow a right-leaning ramp (5.10a R) to a belay stance with a 2-bolt anchor. **Pitch 2:** Move right and jam up a short finger crack (5.11a) to a good ledge with a 2-bolt rap anchor.

11. South Face (5.10a) **Pitch 1:** Layback a short right-facing dihedral (5.8) and hand traverse left (5.10a) to a ledge. Move left past bolts and follow a ledge system up left to a crack (5.6) and a belay ledge with a bolt and piton. **Pitch 2:** Climb directly (5.7) to a right-angling ramp and corner. Climb the ramp to a tricky face traverse up left (5.9) to a crack. Continue (5.9) to a belay ledge. **Pitch 3:** Finish up *Jackson's Wall*. Climb a crack, then work left and back right up a corner system. Finish up left over ledges to the top.

12. Athlete's Feat (5.11a) Superb and sustained crack climb. Begin at a pointed boulder beside the road. **Pitch 1:** Crank the crux mantle (5.11a) onto a sloping slab and belay at a

In 1964 the great Yosemite climber Royal Robbins, belayed by Pat Ament, made the first free ascent of *Athlete's Feat*. The route, with its five short pitches including four 5.10 pitches, was the most sustained free climb in the United States at that time. Royal wore Tretorn tennis shoes from Switzerland for the ascent.

2-bolt anchor. **Pitch 2:** Layback the overhanging corner above (5.10d) and jam an easier crack to a belay. **Pitch 3:** Layback or jam a corner crack (5.10b/c) for 45 feet to a belay. **Pitch 4:** Work up a tricky corner (5.10b) to a 2-bolt anchor on the left. Make two 100-foot rappels to the ground or do **Pitch 5:** Climb a crack (5.9+) above the belay or move left and climb a corner (5.8) to the summit.

13. Country Club Crack (5.11b/c) Boulder Canyon classic crack climb. **Pitch 1:** Grab polished holds (5.11c) past 2 bolts. This boulder start is the route crux. Jam an awkward hand crack (5.9) to The Bar, an airy belay ledge. 65 feet. **Pitch 2:** Jam a sustained hand crack (5.10) to a roof. Pull the roof and jam an insecure finger crack (5.11a) to easier rock and a 2-bolt anchor up right. **Descent:** Rappel with double ropes, or rappel with a 200-foot (60-meter) rope and swing over to *Athlete's Feat*'s second anchors.

Eldorado Canyon State Park

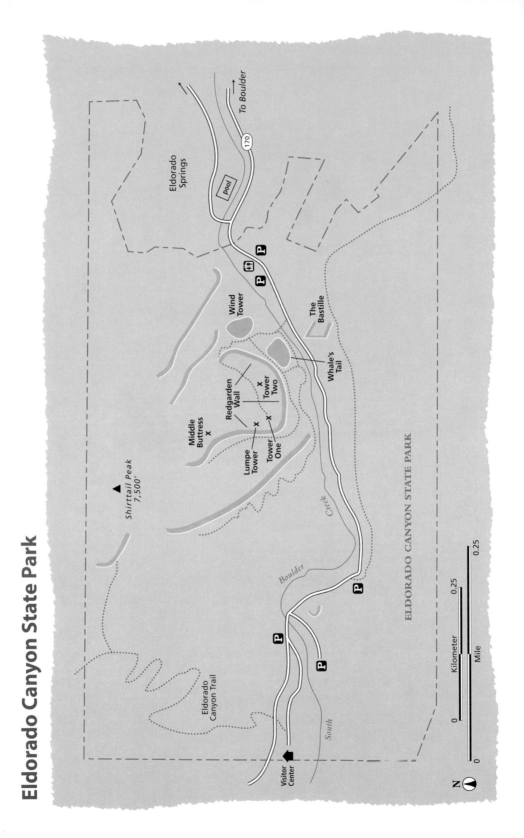

2.

Eldorado Canyon State Park

Eldorado Canyon is simply one of America's most famous and best climbing areas. Its towering sandstone cliffs sweep up from South Boulder Creek with a stunning natural geometry of sheer walls, sharp arêtes, wide roofs, and pointed summits. Hundreds of climbing routes and variations ascend the colorful faces, offering the rock climber a wide variety of challenges of all grades, from chimney and gully climbs to overhanging face routes that test the limits of human ability. The canyon and cliffs are protected by Eldorado Canyon State Park.

Eldorado Canyon, usually called Eldo, is a traditional-style climbing area. Most of the routes, especially those described here, are well protected with gear and only occasional bolts. The rock quality is impeccable, with a firm, compact surface studded with flakes and crisp edges, rounded cobbles, and intermittent crack systems. While Eldo is a traditional area, most of the routes are face climbs rather than crack climbs. Expect to find delicate face moves, tricky traverses, stems up shallow corners, and short jam cracks. Descent off the cliffs is by rappelling from bolt anchors and trees or downclimbing slabs.

Most people first encounter Eldorado Canyon rock by climbing on Wind Tower, Whale's Tail, or The Bastille near the canyon's east mouth. These cliffs offer fabulous climbing opportunities. Sample the smaller crags, then venture onto the complex 700-foot-high Redgarden Wall and climb some of the longer classic lines like *T2* and *The Yellow Spur*. You won't soon forget the feeling of standing atop one of Redgarden's pointed summits after an afternoon of climbing and feeling the last warmth of the evening sun on your face.

Eldorado Canyon is climbable year-round. Spring and autumn are the best months, with generally warm sunny days. It can be very windy in the canyon in the springtime. Summers are good but can be very hot, particularly on the south-facing cliffs. The Bastille and other cliffs on the south side of the canyon are a good bet if it's hot. Winter days can be brilliant, with warm sunshine on Redgarden Wall, but it can also be cold, snowy, and windy.

Getting there: From Denver, drive north on Interstate 25 and exit west on US 36 toward Boulder. Follow US 36 to the exit for CO 170. Exit here and follow CO 170 to CO 93 just south of Boulder. Continue west on CO 170 to the town of Eldorado Springs. From Boulder, drive south on CO 93 (Broadway) to its junction with CO 170 at a stop light. Turn right (west) onto CO 170 and drive a few miles to the town of Eldorado Springs.

Bump through Eldorado Springs on a rough dirt road to the Eldorado Canyon State Park entrance. Pay an entry fee to enter the park. Park your vehicle in one of the lots just past the entry kiosk. Don't park in the town outside the park. It's illegal unless you're a resident, and you will get a ticket. Annual park passes are available.

Ivy Baldwin is Eldorado's most famous aerialist. Between 1906 and 1948 the stuntman walked a high wire between The Bastille and Wind Tower without a safety rope 87 times, with his last walk on his 82nd birthday. The wire, 582 feet above the canyon floor and stretching 635 feet across the canyon, was removed in 1974.

THE BASTILLE

The Bastille rises sharply above the creek and road on Eldorado Canyon's south side just west of the main parking area. The 300-foot-high cliff offers excellent routes with great climbing and easy accessibility.

Finding the crag: Park in the main parking area near the canyon entrance. Walk west on the road for a couple minutes to the obvious cliff rising above the road on the left. The west face routes are accessed by a trail up the steep, loose gully below the face. Find the trail's start just west of the crag.

Descent: To descend from the summit, work south along the ridgetop to the old railroad cut behind The Bastille. The safest way from here is to walk west almost a mile on level Fowler Trail to its intersection with the canyon road. Otherwise descend steep talus slopes on the west side of the crag. This descent is loose. Take care not to dislodge any rocks on your partners or climbers below. Numerous accidents have occurred on this descent. Use caution!

1. Werk Supp (5.9+) Good shady route. Begin from the road. **Pitch 1:** Excellent. Climb cracks and flakes for 30 feet, then layback a flake to a stance. Climb a finger crack (5.8+) to a sloping ledge with a 2-bolt anchor. 150 feet. **Pitch 2:** Move the belay or traverse left 15 feet on the ledge to an obvious right-angling crack. Climb the crack, beginning with

Creighton Chute grabs a flake on the first pitch of the mega-classic *Bastille Crack* in Eldorado Canyon.
PHOTO ROB KEPLEY

scramble off backside

continue to summit

scramble off

3

5

XX

1

park road

2 4

a squeeze chimney to a hand crack (5.9+). Belay on a ledge. For a third pitch, jam the *March of Dimes* finger crack (5.10c) above the ledge. **Descent:** Scramble east down ramps and shelves. From the top of pitch 1, make two single-rope rappels from bolts to the ground. **Rack:** Sets of Stoppers and TCUs; cams to #3 Camalot, including two #3, two #2.5, and a #4 Camalot.

2. Bastille Crack (5.7) Mega-classic crack climb that is one of Colorado's most popular routes. Usually done in five pitches to ease rope drag. It's usually busy, especially on weekends. Watch for loose rocks dislodged from above. Begin from the road below the obvious crack. **Pitch 1:** Climb a thin flake and step left into the crack. Layback and jam the crack (5.7) to a stance with two bolts. Put gear in the flake and crack before stepping into it. Ground falls occur here. 65 feet. *The Northcutt Start* (5.10d) climbs a crack left of the pitch with a crux traverse at the top. **Pitch 2:** Jam and layback the crack (5.6 and 5.7) for 90 feet to a good belay ledge. The first two pitches are easily combined. **Pitch 3:** Climb twin cracks (5.7) up a steep headwall for 45 feet to a sloping belay ledge. **Pitch 4:** Traverse down left to a broken corner system. Climb moderate rock (5.7) to another sloping stance. **Pitch 5:** Climb ledges and short walls to a chimney (5.4) and the summit. **Rack:** Medium to large Stoppers and cams to 4 inches.

3. Outer Space (5.10c R) Exposed, excellent climbing. Start by climbing the first two pitches of *Bastille Crack* to a ledge. **Pitch 1:** Diagonal right 35 feet up a ramp to a hard move (5.9) to the base of a left-facing red dihedral. Work up the steep dihedral (5.9+ and 5.10a cruxes) to a sloping ramp. Belay up right below an arching corner. **Pitch 2:** Wild climbing! Climb steep rock up left below the corner to a piton. Undercling left (5.10c R) around an edge, then climb a left-facing corner (5.9) to a left-leaning crack. Grab big holds on easier rock to the summit. Use runners to avoid rope drag. **Rack:** Sets of Stoppers, TCUs, and cams to 3 inches.

4. Direct North Face (5.11a R) Excellent combination of *Wide Country*, *XM*, and *Outer Space*, making a steep, spectacular direct climb up the north face. Expect sustained 5.10 climbing, one 5.11 move, and tricky pro. Start just right of *Bastille Crack*. **Pitch 1:** Climb flakes to the base of a left-facing corner. Climb the corner (5.9 R) to a stance, then up another short corner to a bolt. Step left (5.11a) to a sloping stance. Face climb up left (5.9 R) to a small roof and climb up right (5.10b) to a shallow vertical corner and a 2-bolt belay shelf. 100 feet. **Pitch 2:** Layback up left (5.10c) past fixed pitons to a committing mantle onto a narrow shelf. Climb easier terrain to a ledge. **Pitch 3:** Climb to the base of a nice red dihedral. Stem and

jam up the dihedral (5.9+ and 5.10a), then up right to *Outer Space*'s ramp belay. **Pitch 4:** Climb exposed rock up left below a corner. Undercling left (5.10c R) around an edge, then climb a left-facing corner (5.9) to a left-angling crack. Grab big holds on easier rock to the top. Use runners to avoid rope drag. **Rack:** Sets of RPs, Stoppers, and TCUs; cams to 3 inches.

5. West Buttress (5.9) Classic varied climbing on the west face. Scramble up talus and start on boulders. **Pitch 1:** Climb up and hand traverse left (5.7) to a vertical crack. Jam for a few moves (5.9), then step left to easier rock. Climb straight up (5.6 R) and rejoin the crack when the angle eases. Or jam the sustained crack (5.10b) to the belay. Above the crack, climb to a 2-bolt belay stance beneath an off-width crack. **Pitch 2:** Work up the wide crack to a bolt (5.9), then chimney above to a ledge with a 2-bolt anchor atop a big flake. **Pitch 3:** Climb up left along the ledge, then climb a chimney (5.7) past an overhang to a good ledge. Cruise to the summit up an easy chimney or a slab (5.4) to the right. **Rack:** Sets of Stoppers, TCUs, and cams.

6. Hair City (5.9 R) One of Eldo's best climbs! Route climbs the outside of the giant flake right of *West Buttress*. **Pitch 1:** Climb up left into a thin corner with a fixed piton and mantle onto a narrow shelf. Climb straight up

past a couple bolts (5.8+) to a runout juggy section (5.7 R) to a bulge at the base of the flake. Grab edges (5.8+) up left and finish with thin moves to a belay atop the flake from a 2-bolt anchor. 140 feet. **Pitch 2:** Climb up left on broken rock to the middle crack system. Crux moves (5.9) lead over a steep bulge to a rest. Pull up big flakes (sling for pro) to a good belay ledge. 50 feet. **Pitch 3:** Pull over a short bulge and grab great edges (5.5) to the top. **Rack:** RPs, set of Stoppers with extra mediums, TCUs, and extra slings.

7. West Arête (5.8+) Classic, elegant, and fun. Start uphill from *Hair City* on a terrace below a blunt arête. **Pitch 1:** Climb up left (5.6) to a couple short cracks. Pull past them on slick edges (5.8+) and head toward a long, thin crack up the arête. Climb the crack to easier rock and a belay stance. **Pitch 2:** Squeeze up a tight chimney (5.6) on the right side of a big flake to a

According to state park statistics, the ten most dangerous routes in Eldorado Canyon are the following: *Bastille Crack, Calypso, Tagger, Redguard, Werk Supp, Rewritten, The Bulge, Touch and Go, Ruper,* and *Recon.* Most serious accidents occur to novice climbers on moderate routes (5.6–5.9).

2-bolt anchor on top. **Pitch 3:** Three options. Finish up *Hair City* or *West Buttress* or do a third pitch. Climb broken rock to an overhung crack and sling a big chockstone. Swing up right along the steep crack (5.8+) and pass the lip. Finish up fun rock (5.6) to a belay ledge. **Pitch 4:** Climb directly up good, juggy rock (5.5) to the top. **Rack:** Sets of Stoppers, TCUs, and cams.

WIND TOWER

Wind Tower, directly north of the lower parking lot, is a 300-foot-high formation that offers lots of great climbs on its steep south face and its slabby west wall. The classic routes up the west face are some of Colorado's most popular climbs, including *West Ridge, Calypso,* and *Recon.* These routes can be very busy on the weekend. Come early or on weekdays to avoid crowds. Also wear a helmet and watch for falling rocks dislodged by climbers above.

Finding the crag: Park in the lower parking area near the canyon mouth. Hike west up the road and cross a footbridge over South Boulder Creek. Follow a trail right along the cliff base to access the south face or hike up a trail that heads up right from the bridge to the base of the west face.

Descent: From the summit, scramble northeast to a notch. Make a short rappel from a 2-bolt anchor west to a talus slope or downclimb (5.4). Below, follow a trail down a gully

on the west side of Wind Tower. If you don't climb to the top, rappel from bolt anchors atop *Recon*'s second pitch or *Calypso*'s first pitch with a 200-foot (60-meter) rope. Don't knock rocks on others below if you're rappelling.

1. Wind Ridge (5.6 or 5.7+) Fun classic climb. Begin from a ledge directly below the ridge. **Pitch 1:** Two options. Climb up left on a ramp (5.6), then traverse back right to the ridge. Or climb a large flake above the ledge (couple 5.7+ moves) and climb to the ridge. Pull easier rock to a belay ledge. **Pitch 2:** Step right on a shelf. Jam a crack (5.5) to hand jams (5.6) up another crack. Finish at a ledge. **Pitch 3:** Grab a flake and pull over a roof (5.6), then climb past a large tree to a belay ledge. **Descent:** Scramble northeast to a notch and a 50-foot rappel. **Rack:** Set of Stoppers and cams to 3 inches.

2. Calypso (5.6) Great climbing. Begin at a huge boulder. **Pitch 1:** Chimney behind the boulder (5.6) or traverse right (5.5) into a right-facing dihedral. Fun moves lead up the dihedral to a roof. Layback up right (5.6) on slippery rock to a ledge and 2-bolt belay anchor to the right. **Pitch 2:** Climb a thin 20-foot crack up left (5.6), then climb easily to a belay ledge. **Pitch 3:** Climb right into a corner (5.5) and then up left to the summit. **Descent:** Downclimb north from the summit or rappel 100 feet from the top of pitch 1.

Wind Tower

scramble
off back

1

2

3

100'

XX

XX

90'

.4

.4

4

5

3. Reggae (5.8) Recommended second pitch for *Calypso*. **Pitch 1:** Climb *Calypso's* first pitch to the belay. **Pitch 2:** Step right to the base of a prominent right-facing dihedral. Climb the dihedral (5.6) to a finger crack (5.8) up the left side of a flake. Near the top, move right to a belay ledge above the dihedral. **Pitch 3:** Climb easy rock to the summit.

4. Recon (5.4) 3 pitches. Easy climbing up a crack system. Start below an obvious crack. **Pitch 1:** Climb a left-facing corner to a crack (5.4) and belay on a ledge. 140 feet. **Pitch 2:** Many options. Best is to move left to the base of a chimney. Climb the chimney (5.4) to a ledge belay. **Pitch 3:** Climb onto the south ridge (5.4) and cruise to the top. **Descent:** Downclimb north or make two rappels down the route from the top of pitch 2.

5. The Yellow Traverse to Metamorphosis (5.9+ R) A great combination up the vertical south face. Start by hiking along the south face's base to a left-leaning ramp near the right corner. Climb the ramp (3rd class) 100 feet to a belay atop a V-shaped pedestal. **Pitch 1:** *The Yellow Traverse.* Climb down left to a small ledge. Traverse up left (5.9-) on poorly protected rock below a black groove to a belay ledge. **Pitch 2:** *Metamorphosis.* Climb vertical rock right from the belay. Work up a left-facing corner (5.9+), then up

left past old bolts. Climb up right past a bolt and a flake (5.9+), then pull a bulge (5.9) to a left-leaning ramp to a tree belay at the top. Finish with a scrambling pitch to the summit.

WHALE'S TAIL
Whale's Tail, opposite The Bastille, has excellent beginner routes on its slabby west face. The sunny 200-foot wall is also good for toproping and for moderate leaders with good gear placements and safe climbing.

Finding the crag: From the parking area at the canyon entrance, walk up the road and cross the footbridge over the creek. Go left on a trail along the creek's north side to the cliff. For the described routes, hike past a cave and concrete platform, then scramble up the slopes above to the west face.

Descent: See climb descriptions.

1. Clementine (5.5) Start up left of the concrete platform. **Pitch 1:** Climb a left-facing corner for 15 feet, traverse right (hard to protect), and climb a bulge to a ledge. **Pitch 2:** Climb easy terrain to an exposed crack. End below the top. **Descent:** Scramble 10 feet up left and rappel 100 feet from anchors.

2. West Dihedral (5.4) Fine beginner lead. Start by scrambling right (4th class) from a gully to a belay ledge. Stem, layback, and face climb up a left-facing dihedral to a crux (5.4). End at a belay with

Roxanne Raymundo leads *West Crack*
on the Whale's Tail, Eldorado Canyon.
PHOTO MATTHEW KELLEY

a cable anchor. **Descent:** Rappel 100 feet back to the starting ledge.

3. West Crack (5.2) Obvious crack up a slab. Begin by scrambling right (4th class) from a gully to a good ledge below the crack. Climb the crack to a fixed cable around boulders at the top. 100 feet. **Descent:** Rappel 100 feet back to the ledge.

REDGARDEN WALL

The Redgarden Wall is Eldorado's biggest wall. The 700-foot-high cliff, dominating the canyon's north side, is a complex wall with big ramps, sharp arêtes, roofs, vertical faces, and four distinct summits. The cliff offers lots of classic face climbing routes from one to eight pitches long. Expect fun climbing and generally good protection on all of these traditional-style routes.

Finding the crag: To reach Redgarden Wall from the road, cross the footbridge over the creek and turn left (west) on Streamside Trail below the Whale's Tail. At a concrete slab on the far side of the Whale's Tail, turn right and scramble up a boulder field to the base of the wall below *C'est La Vie*. A trail follows the cliff base west from here, providing access to the routes above the Lower Ramp and the west flank of the wall. Alternatively, reach the west face by walking upstream (west) on Streamside Trail past the Whale's Tail. An access trail begins just past a low buttress below

the Lower Ramp and winds uphill to the face. Keep on the trails and don't cut switchbacks.

Descent: The descent from the top is difficult to find. The East Slabs descent is the easiest way off. From the top, scramble east and southeast down steep gullies below the notches between the summits and onto slick east-sloping slabs. Descend the slabs into a narrow wooded gully. Downclimbing is necessary in places, particularly if you get off the easiest route. Eventually drop into a broad, boulder-choked gully that leads southeast between Hawk-Eagle Ridge and Redgarden's East Slabs. Follow a rocky trail down the gully past Wind Tower to the creek and bridge. This descent is very dangerous in the dark or when wet. Use extreme caution and rope up if necessary. Fatalities have occurred on the descent.

A common descent from the Upper Ramp makes two rappels from bolted anchors below *The Naked Edge*. Descend the ramp to its eastern base and traverse east around a corner to rappel bolts on a ledge below *The Naked Edge*. Make a 75-foot rappel from these anchors to another bolted rappel anchor. Make a 150-foot rappel to the ground, or two 75-foot rappels using anchors at the end of *T2*'s first pitch.

From the top of Tower 1 and Lumpe Tower, make four single-rope rappels down the west face. Downclimb to a notch between *Swanson*

Arête and Tower One (*The Yellow Spur*). **Rappel 1:** From a threaded anchor at the notch, rappel 85 feet to a ledge with a tree. **Rappel 2:** Rappel 105 feet from the tree to large Red Ledge. Scramble north on the ledge under the base of *Swanson Arête* to a 2-bolt anchor at the top of the West Chimney. **Rappels 3 and 4:** Make two short rappels from bolt anchors to the ground. Use extreme caution not to knock rocks off. People are below.

1. C'est La Vie (5.9) Excellent. On the lower right side of the face. While the route has two pitches, it's best to climb the excellent first pitch and rap off. Start on a ledge below a right-angling dihedral. **Pitch 1:** Climb a shallow corner to a flake. Step right (5.9) and layback a left-facing flake to a notch. Pull over the notch (5.8) and either climb a tricky slab up left (5.9-) to a 2-bolt anchor or climb directly up a slab and arête to a high 2-bolt anchor. A better anchor is to the right. **Descent:** Rappel 150 feet from the top anchor to the base.

2. Anthill Direct (5.9 R) Classic climbing and tricky routefinding. Instead of the old first pitch below a left-angling black ramp, climb *Touch and Go.* Start below a roof. **Pitch 1:** Climb under the roof, then up left on flakes (5.9) to a corner. Climb a V-slot to a finger crack (5.7) to a ramp. Step left to a corner and climb it (5.8) to a 2-bolt anchor on a ledge. **Pitch 2:** Climb up

right onto a pretty slab (5.4), head up to a crack (5.6), and pull over an obvious, exposed overhang (5.8) to a good belay. **Pitch 3:** Short pitch. Head diagonally left up across a run-out black slab (5.6 R) to a ledge belay. **Pitch 4:** Climb up right (5.5) to a thin, right-facing corner. Climb a fun, vertical crack (5.5) and then angle left to a belay stance below a bulge. **Pitch 5:** Climb up right under the bulge to a dihedral. Layback an exposed crack (5.9) in the dihedral to easier rock and a belay ledge atop the South Buttress. **Descent:** Head northwest across easy slabs above the wall to the East Slabs descent.

3. Touch and Go (5.9) A superb and popular line that makes a great start to *Anthill Direct.* It's climbed so much the holds are polished. Begin around a corner and uphill from *Redguard* below a thin, slanted roof. Climb under the roof and up left on flakes (5.9) into a short, left-facing corner. Work into an upside-down V-slot and jam a good finger crack (5.7) to a sloping ramp. Traverse left to an excellent right-facing corner. Jam, layback, and stem up the corner (5.8) to a ledge with two bolts. **Descent:** Rappel 125 feet with two ropes to the ground from here or continue up to *Anthill Direct* or *The Naked Edge.*

4. Bolting for Glory (5.10a) Variation to *Touch and Go.* At the sloping ramp on *Touch and Go,* climb directly up a

steep slab (5.10a) past three bolts to the 2-bolt belay ledge. **Descent:** Rappel 125 feet.

5. The Naked Edge (5.11b) *The Naked Edge,* one of Colorado's most famous climbs, offers everything a great route should have: lots of exposure, superb position, hard climbing, and a spectacular direct line. To reach the start, climb *Touch and Go* to its belay ledge and then work left up a sloping ramp to a bolted, sloping belay ledge directly below the *Edge.* **Pitch 1:** Jam and stem up a thin finger crack just right of the edge (5.11a) for 75 feet to a stance with two bolts. **Pitch 2:** Spectacular and unnerving. Face climb the left side of a slab above the belay (some fixed pro) to a leaning roof. Traverse left around the arête (5.9+) and jam a thin crack (5.10b) to an exposed stance. **Pitch 3:** Follow the edge (5.6) to a niche, step right to an awkward mantle (5.8+), and work up right to a sloping ledge beneath an overhanging chimney. **Pitch 4:** Jam strenuous cracks and corners (5.11a) to the top of a chimney slot. Exit over the roof capping the slot (5.10c) to a small,

Jim Collins made an audacious free-solo ascent of *The Naked Edge* in the summer of 1978—after falling off the 5.11 crux on five of his six roped ascents of the route.

Nick Chan getting maximum exposure on the amazing and storied Eldo route *The Naked Edge*.

broken ledge. **Pitch 5:** Continue up a shallow, continuous corner (5.11a) to the right side of the hanging prow. Jam or layback a scary, strenuous, overhanging hand and fist crack (5.10d) to a small stance on the right. **Pitch 6:** Climb up and left around the arête and motor up easy slabs to the summit. **Descent:** Scramble northeast to the descent downclimb. **Rack:** Lots of small pro including RPs and Stoppers, and Friends to #4.

6. T2 (5.11a) 6 to 8 pitches. An Eldo classic. Highly recommended. The starting bouldery moves are out of character with the rest of *T2*. Start uphill from *Touch and Go* beneath a

In 1959 Layton Kor invited Gerry Roach to try a new route he called *T2* up Redgarden Wall. Layton led the entire climb, sometimes pulling on the rope to make Gerry move faster. Roach described the sixth pitch, which Kor led without pitons: "Only when I protested did he place one. When I reached it I plucked it out with my fingers . . . I hollered up to Layton, 'Hey! This pin is just sitting here!' Layton shouted down, 'Yeah, well I didn't want you to get too worried, since you might report me to your mom!'"

long roof with a drilled piton above it. **Pitch 1:** Pull over the roof on strenuous flakes (5.11a) to a fixed piton. Leaders should be confident, otherwise use a shoulder stand or stick-clip the pin. Climb up right on steep but moderate rock (a spot of 5.8) to a bolted belay on a left-angling ramp. **Pitch 2:** Start a few feet west up the ramp and follow a shallow, grungy chimney (5.8) to a stance in a slot cave. **Pitch 3:** Work diagonally left onto the right side of the Upper Ramp. This short pitch can be combined with pitch 2 for a long lead. **Pitch 4:** Begin about 75 feet west up the ramp below a shallow black gully. Climb the grooved gully (5.8) to a narrow shelf 60 feet up. A scary traverse (5.8) bumps left to an excellent finger crack (5.9) that arches up and left. Belay at a small stance in the crack. **Pitch 5:** Angle left up the widening crack to a huge right-facing dihedral. Climb the slabby ramp on the right side of the dihedral (5.7) to an airy belay below a large roof. **Pitch 6:** Climb left out the overhanging side of the dihedral (5.9 R) along a rotten red band with bad fall potential. Belay up left on a groove/ramp. **Pitch 7 and 8:** Follow the left-angling groove/ramp to a large tree in the saddle west of Tower Two. **Descent:** Scramble down the East Slabs descent.

7. Rosy Crucifixion (5.10a) Must-do classic with airy situations. Begin by scrambling up the Lower Ramp, a

wide ramp (3rd class) west of a long angling roof. From the ramp top, chimney behind a large block to a short corner to a narrow, angling ramp and a belay shelf. **Pitch 1:** Traverse straight right (exposed 5.10a) above a large roof, passing four pitons, to an exposed belay in a corner. **Pitch 2:** Climb a crack system (5.9+) for 45 feet to a bolted belay. **Pitch 3:** Work straight up for 40 feet, then make a tricky downward traverse (5.9) to the right to a good belay ledge. **Pitch 4:** Climb easy rock to the Upper Ramp. **Descent:** Two rappels from the base of *The Naked Edge* to the ground.

8. Ruper (5.8) 6 pitches. Mega-classic with fun climbing. Many climb the first three pitches and rap off. To start, scramble 200 feet up the Lower Ramp (3rd class) and belay on a ledge above a large boulder above the ramp. **Pitch 1:** Climb easy cracks and corners above the ramp to a good ledge. **Pitch 2:** Traverse right 20 feet to the base of the Ruper Crack. Struggle up the off-width crack (5.8) for 75 feet, then step right to a ledge. **Pitch 3:** The Ruper Traverse—classic Eldo pitch. Traverse right across a series of shallow corners (5.7) to a left-facing corner that leads to the Upper Ramp. Belay from a tree. **Descent:** Make two rappels from the ledge below *The Naked Edge* or continue up the last three pitches. **Pitch 4:** Start by hiking down the ramp to the right side of a cave. Climb a left-facing corner (5.6) and work left up a vertical

wall (5.8), then diagonal right into the corner. Continue the steep corner (5.6) to a belay atop a flake. **Pitch 5:** Climb the corner above (5.6) for 100 feet. Belay beneath a large red roof. **Pitch 6:** Traverse up left (5.8) past fixed pitons and hand traverse left under the roof. Diagonal up left on easier rock to a saddle between Towers One and Two. **Descent:** From the Upper Ramp: Make two rappels down right of *Vertigo*. Scramble west to the top of the Upper Ramp; downclimb on the right to a 2-bolt rappel anchor by a tree. Rappel 65 feet to a stance with bolts and chains. Rappel 95 feet to Vertigo Ledge. Scramble north on the ledge. From the top of route: Scramble northeast and downclimb the East Slabs. **Rack:** Sets of Stoppers, TCUs, and cams to 4 inches; #4 Camalot useful.

9. Grand Giraffe (5.10a) Superb Eldo classic. Begin at the start of *Ruper*. **Pitch 1:** Follow *Ruper*'s first pitch up corners to a belay alcove below a flake. **Pitch 2:** Climb up left on a steep

> Layton Kor and George Hurley made the first ascent of *Grand Giraffe* in 1960. The name, Hurley recalls, "was a takeoff on the Grandes Jorasses and a way of debunking ourselves and our efforts in a canyon in the foothills of the gentle Rockies."

wall to a leaning crack. Climb the crack (5.8+) to a belay ledge. **Pitch 3:** Climb a groove straight up to a right-facing corner (5.4). Belay below an obvious off-width crack over a roof. **Pitch 4:** Climb the off-width to a strenuous bulge (5.10a) and belay on the Upper Ramp. **Pitch 5:** Begin on the ramp's north side at the left edge of an arching cave. Climb up vertical rock (5.6) for 80 feet, then traverse right and climb to a belay stance. **Pitch 6:** Diagonal up left on rock (5.6) for 20 feet, then angle right on jugs for 100 feet to a saddle. **Descent:** From the Upper Ramp: Make two rappels down right of *Vertigo*. Scramble west to the top of the Upper Ramp; downclimb on the right to a 2-bolt rappel anchor by a tree. Rappel 65 feet to a stance with bolts and chains. Rappel 95 feet to Vertigo Ledge. Scramble north on the ledge. From the top of route: Scramble northeast and descend the East Slabs. **Rack:** Sets of Stoppers, TCUs, and cams to 4 inches.

10. Super Slab (5.10d R) One of Eldo's best. Start from the top of the Lower Ramp and go west on a ledge past a tree. **Pitch 1:** Climb to a flake/roof (5.10c), then work left into a shallow corner and climb for 50 feet to a left traverse (5.9) to a belay below a corner. **Pitch 2:** Climb a left-facing corner (5.6) to a ledge on the right. 50 feet. **Pitch 3:** Climb to a fixed piton. Traverse left around an exposed edge (5.8) to the base of Super Slab. Climb (5.8+) to a belay shelf. **Pitch 4:** Climb to a bolt, then face climb (5.10d) to a shallow, left-facing corner. Work up right on edges (5.10 R) to a good hold. Climb scary rock (5.9) to a narrow roof (5.9); pass it on the left (5.9) and climb easier terrain (5.8) to the Upper Ramp. **Descent:** Make two rappels down right of *Vertigo*. From the top, downclimb to a 2-bolt rappel anchor. Rappel 65 feet to a stance with bolts and chains. Rappel 95 feet to Vertigo Ledge. Scramble north on the ledge. **Rack:** Set of Stoppers and cams to 2 inches; RPs and Lowe Balls useful on crux pitch.

11. Vertigo (5.11b) Exposed and pumpy. To approach, follow directions to *The Yellow Spur*. Scramble south on Vertigo Ledge to its far right side. **Pitch 1:** Climb a left-facing dihedral, then a right-facing dihedral (5.9) to a ledge. **Pitch 2:** Climb up left over a bulge (5.9+) to easier rock. Continue up right to a belay with bolts above a dihedral. **Pitch 3:** Work up an overhanging, right-facing dihedral (5.11b) to a belay up left. **Pitch 4:** Jam a crack over a big roof (5.11a). Finish a steep crack to the top of the Upper Ramp. **Descent:** Make two rappels down right of *Vertigo*. Downclimb to a 2-bolt rappel anchor by a tree. Rappel 65 feet to a stance with bolts and chains. Rappel 95 feet to Vertigo Ledge. Scramble north on the ledge. **Rack:** Standard Eldo rack with small Aliens.

12. The Yellow Spur (5.10a) One of Colorado's best climbs. Approach from the Streamside Trail. Walk west on the trail to a path that zigzags up to the west face of Redgarden Wall. Scramble up slabs to a ledge that runs along the wall's base. Begin in trees below the roofs. **Pitch 1:** Begin below the largest roof. Climb a right-facing corner (5.9) to a roof and traverse left to its left edge. A direct start (5.10a R) climbs to the left edge of the roof from the ledge. Turn the left side of the roof (5.8) and angle up right on easier rock to a belay stance. **Pitch 2:** Diagonal up left to a right-facing dihedral (5.8). Climb it, then step left on a horizontal band to a belay. **Pitch 3:** Work up a corner (5.7) to a ledge, pull over a small roof (5.7), and stem up a dihedral (5.8) to a ledge. **Pitch 4:** Traverse right on the ledge. Climb a huge dihedral (5.4) to a belay below a big roof. **Pitch 5:** Hand traverse right under the roof to a move around an arête (5.8). Climb a left-facing corner (5.8) to a belay stance on the ridge. **Pitch 6:** Jam a thin crack to a step right onto a vertical wall. Face climb up right (sustained 5.9) past pitons to a stance atop a flake. Continue up right on sustained face climbing (5.9 and a bit of 5.10a) to a thin corner. Easier climbing leads to a belay on the arête. If you chicken out at the final crux, take the *Robbins Traverse* left from the flake stance. Traverse up left to a headwall (5.7). Continue to the belay stance on the ridge. **Pitch**

7: Follow a spectacular exposed arête (5.6 R) to the summit of Tower One. **Descent:** Make four single-rope rappels. Downclimb (5.4) south to a notch between *Swanson Arête* and Tower One (*The Yellow Spur*). **Rappel 1:** From a threaded anchor at the notch, rappel 85 feet to a ledge with a tree. **Rappel 2:** Rappel 105 feet from the tree to large Red Ledge. Scramble north on the ledge under the base of *Swanson Arête* to a 2-bolt anchor at the top of the West Chimney. **Rappels 3 and 4:** Make two short rappels from bolt anchors to the ground. Use extreme caution not to knock rocks off! People are below. Alternatively, do the East Slabs descent. **Rack:** Sets of Stoppers and cams to #3 Camalot.

13. Swanson Arête (5.5) Classic beginner route. Watch for loose rock. Locate the arête above and start below the West Chimney. Alternatively, do the first pitch of *Rewritten*. **Pitch 1:** Climb up the West Chimney (5.5), which is easy but a bit grungy. Start left of the West Chimney and climb up a corner, then move right into the chimney and head up to Red Ledge. Watch for loose rock up high. Scramble up right on the ledge and belay below the arête. **Pitch 2:** Work up parallel cracks (5.4) right of the arête to a belay stance. **Pitch 3:** Climb up through a slot and make a short traverse down right. Pull over a small bulge above (5.5) and belay by a tree. **Pitch 4:** Climb an excellent crack

system and dihedral to a traverse around a roof (5.5). Finish up a short corner to the tower summit. **Descent:** Make four single-rope rappels. Down-climb (5.4) south to a notch between *Swanson Arête* and Tower One (*The Yellow Spur*). **Rappel 1:** From a threaded anchor at the notch, rappel 85 feet to a ledge with a tree. **Rappel 2:** Rappel 105 feet from the tree to large Red Ledge. Scramble north on the ledge under the base of *Swanson Arête* to a 2-bolt anchor at the top of the West Chimney. **Rappels 3 and 4:** Make two short rappels from bolt anchors to the ground. Use extreme caution not to knock rocks off! People are below. **Rack:** RPs, set of Stoppers, and cams to 3 inches.

14. The Great Zot (5.8) First two pitches. While the route goes to the top, the first two pitches are a great linkup for either *Swanson Arête* or *Rewritten*. Start just left of the West Chimney. **Pitch 1:** Climb a thin crack up a corner (5.5) to a sloping ledge and step left. Work up a steep, flared crack (5.8) with good pro. Above, climb a thin crack (5.6) to a belay stance at a flake below a chimney. **Pitch 2:** To climb *Swanson Arête,* clamber up right on flakes (5.3) to a 2-bolt anchor atop West Chimney. To climb *Rewritten,* follow the description for its second pitch.

15. Rewritten (5.7) Classic and excellent with a great finish. Start

below the West Chimney. **Pitch 1:** Two options. For the first (not shown on the topo), climb a ramp up left to steep rock. Pass a bulge (5.6) on an arête and traverse right to a crack. Climb the crack to a good belay behind a flake. Or climb the excellent right-hand crack (5.8) on *The Great Zot* to the same belay. **Pitch 2:** Climb directly up a broken chimney (5.4) to Red Ledge. Scramble left to an eyebolt anchor. **Pitch 3:** Climb directly up from the belay (5.5), passing some blocks. Work up a chimney to a niche belay stance. **Pitch 4:** Make an exposed but fun hand traverse with tricky footwork (5.6) left across the face, then climb a steep, thin crack (5.7) to an exposed belay stance. **Pitch 5:** Climb the right side of Rubuffat's Arête (5.5), then work up the arête's left side. Finish the upper part on the right side (5.5) to an amazing airy belay stance at The Point atop the arête. Bring slings to tie off horns. **Pitch 6:** Climb cracks in the final wall (5.5) to the summit. Pitches 5 and 6 are easily combined. **Descent:** Scramble off north. From the top, scramble north 500 feet to a cairn on another summit, which is the top of a path that leads west to the base. **Rack:** RPs, set of Stoppers, cams to 3 inches, and extra 2-foot slings for tie-offs.

16. Green Spur (5.9) Excellent and interesting crack climbing. Do in one pitch with a 200-foot (60-meter) rope. Start just left of *Rewritten*. **Pitch**

1: Climb 40 feet up an easy corner to a ledge. **Pitch 2:** Climb a couple parallel cracks until the right one pinches down. Continue up the left crack, which widens into a squeeze chimney/off-width (5.9). Above, jam, stem, and layback up a crack in a gorgeous dihedral (5.9) to a roof, then step right to a good foothold and swing up easier but runout rock to an eyebolt anchor on Red Ledge (same as end of pitch 2 on *Rewritten*). Continue up *Rewritten* or rappel. **Descent:** Rappel with double 200-foot (60-meter) ropes from the eyebolt to the ground. **Rack:** RPs, sets of Stoppers and TCUs, cams to 3 inches, two ropes. Wear helmets to protect from rockfall on *Rewritten*.

The Flatirons

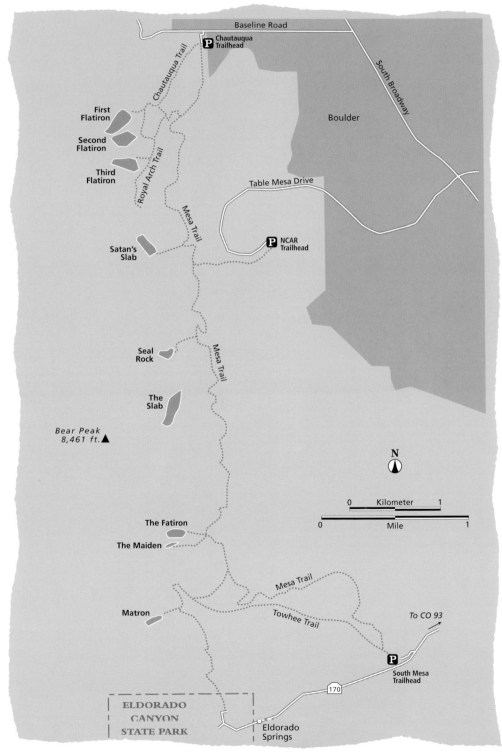

3.

The Flatirons

The Flatirons, a collection of tilted sandstone slabs, faces, and pinnacles, form Boulder's distinctive mountain skyline. The conspicuous cliffs, pasted on a 6-mile escarpment formed by Green Mountain and Boulder Mountain, offer the rock climber hundreds of routes of all difficulties, from long easy scrambles to overhanging 5.14 testpieces. Most of the big cliffs, while appearing monolithic and imposing from town, assume a friendly character up close, with lots of climbing features including grooves, flakes, and cracks on their reasonably angled 50-degree slabs.

Boulder Mountain Park, part of the largest urban park system in Colorado, protects the Flatirons and their scenic beauty. Numerous trails lace the park, allowing easy foot access to all the major cliffs. If you dislike hiking, however, be advised that most of the Flatiron climbs require at least a half hour of walking from the nearest road. Some of the cliffs are closed for raptor nesting from February 1 until July 31. Check with the Boulder Open Space office for details. Closure signs and maps are also posted at the various trailheads.

The Flatiron rock climbs, despite being mostly moderate in difficulty, are still serious routes. Both the First and Third Flatirons are over 1,000 feet high, so climbing them can be a major undertaking for many climbers. Be aware that routefinding can sometimes be difficult, but most of the slabby terrain is easily climbed. Protection can be difficult to find. It's not uncommon to find 50-foot runouts. Retreat can be dangerous since few fixed anchors are found. Be sure to carry extra clothes, food, and water. Watch for lightning on summer afternoons when thunderstorms brew to the west.

A basic rack of climbing gear for the Flatirons includes sets of Stoppers and TCUs, cams to 3 inches, a half-dozen slings with free carabiners, and ten quickdraws. A 200-foot (60-meter rope) is best for stringing pitches together. The easier Flatiron routes are best climbed with a light rack of gear.

Most Flatiron climbs face east, getting lots of morning sun. Expect the best climbing weather in spring and autumn with warm and sunny days. Spring afternoons can be windy. Summer offers excellent weather, although it can get hot and sticky on the slabs. Severe thunderstorms build up on summer afternoons. Plan your climbs for the morning to avoid light-ning. Winter can be fine if the weather is dry. Snow, however, often coats the slabs and melts slowly.

Getting there: The Flatirons are on the east side of Boulder Mountain and Green Mountain on the west side of Boulder. The Flatirons are bor-dered by Flagstaff Mountain on the north and Eldorado Canyon on the south. The climbing routes on Boul-der Mountain on the south are best approached from the South Mesa trailhead on CO 170. The routes on Green Mountain, including the First and Third Flatirons, are approached on Baseline Road and Table Mesa Drive.

To reach the South Mesa trail-head, drive south from Boulder for a couple miles on CO 93 to its inter-section with CO 170. Turn west onto CO 170 and drive 1.7 miles toward Eldorado Canyon State Park. The trail-head is on the right side of the road. It accesses Mesa, Towhee, Homestead, Big Bluestem, South Boulder Creek, and Shadow Canyon Trails. Crags accessed from this trailhead include The Matron, The Maiden, and The Fatiron.

To reach the Chautauqua trail-head, drive west on Baseline Road from US 36 (highway from Denver) and from South Broadway Street (CO 93) to Chautauqua Park on the left (south). Park in a lot on the west side of the park immediately after turning into the park. The Ranger Cottage

visitor center is at the south end of the lot. This trailhead accesses Chau-tauqua, Mesa, Baseline, Bluebell-Baird, Royal Arch, Woods Quarry, and First, Second, and Third Flatiron climbing access trails.

To reach the NCAR (National Cen-ter for Atmospheric Research) trail-head, drive west on Table Mesa Drive until the road ends at a large parking area at NCAR. The trailhead accesses NCAR, Mesa, Skunk Canyon, Mallory Cave, Bear Canyon, Bear Peak West Ridge, Green Bear, and Fern Canyon Trails. Trails start at the north side of the building. Cliffs reached from here include Satan's Slab, the Dinosaur Mountain crags, and Seal Rock.

FIRST FLATIRON

The 1,000-foot-high east-facing First Flatiron yields Boulder's longest routes. The *North Arête* is an easy climb to reach the summit, while the *Direct East Face* is a wonderful adventure. Both climbs have lots of variations because it's easy to get off-route on the moderate terrain. You'll be fine if you pay attention and follow the easi-est line. Bring a small rack with a set of Stoppers and cams to 3 inches. A 200-foot (60-meter) rope works best.

Finding the crag: From Denver and I-25, drive northwest on US 36 to Boulder. After entering Boulder, exit at Baseline Road. Drive west on Baseline Road past Broadway. Con-tinue up a long hill and turn left into Chautauqua Park. Park on the right in

First and Third Flatirons

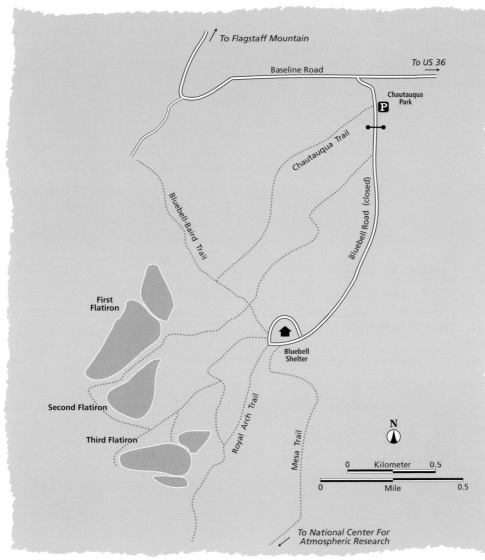

the lot. Hike south up Mesa Trail along the paved Bluebell Road (closed to traffic) to Bluebell Shelter. Head north on Bluebell-Baird Trail to First Flatiron Trail. Follow it west up a steepening ridge before cutting north on a rough path to the base of the Flatiron's east face. The trail continues west to the saddle between the First and Second Flatirons and is used for the descent.

Jason Haas edges up the friendly First Flatiron, which offers the longest climbing routes near Boulder. PHOTO ANDREW BURR

Alternatively, hike southwest up Chautauqua Trail, heading directly uphill toward the First Flatiron. After you reach a junction with the Bluebell-Baird Trail, go left for a short distance and then right on a marked and well-worn climber's trail that leads to the cliff base. Allow thirty to forty-five minutes of hiking to the cliff base.

Descent: Descend from the summit by rappel. Find two eyebolt anchors on the summit and rappel 100 feet to the west. Use a 200-foot (60-meter) rope or double ropes. Hike back to the base on a trail that switchbacks down the slope south of the cliff.

1. North Arête (5.4) Classic beginner climb. Start on the ridge after scrambling around the Flatiron's north side. **Pitch 1:** Begin at a notch. Climb 25 feet and step left onto the east face. Climb to a ledge system below a long roof. 140 feet. **Pitch 2:** Climb to the roof and move left until you can climb to the face above (5.4). Climb easy rock to a belay on the ridge. 150 feet. **Pitch 3:** Climb the arête to a notch. Work up a smooth slab to a belay. 135 feet. **Pitch 4:** Climb up and down across a notch. Work up a groove and then face climb up right to the top of a pillar (5.4), passing the famous quartz knob hold. Continue up the ridge and belay. 155 feet. **Pitch 5:** Scramble up the arête to a notch. Finish with slab moves up a final step to the summit. 150 feet.

2. Direct East Face (II 5.6 R) Excellent—one of Boulder's best. First pitch is hardest. The upper pitches follow *North Arête* from its second step crux. Begin at the lowest point of the east face. **Pitch 1:** Climb past a couple eyebolts, then continue up left on thin climbing (5.6 R) to a belay at a flake. Scant protection, besides three bolts, is found on this sustained pitch. 200 feet. **Pitch 2:** Angle up left on steep rock to a belay ledge. **Pitch 3:** Climb a slab (5.5) to an angling crack to a belay. **Pitch 4:** Ascend straight up the steepening headwall above on excellent holds (5.4) to a huge belay ledge. **Pitch 5:** From the ledge, angle up left to a belay stance below an obvious chimney slot. **Pitches 6 to 8:** Stem the slot (5.5) and continue up a gully to the skyline ridge. Join the *North Arête* here. Climb the arête for a couple pitches, either climbing and belaying or simul-climbing.

3. Fandango (II 5.5) Fun climbing and a good alternative if the *Direct East Face* is busy. Many variations are found; follow your nose to stay on course. This description is for a 200-foot (60-meter) rope. Hike up left on a trail along the south side of the face, then scramble right to the base and left of overlaps to a large boulder. Begin below a large roof about 90 feet above. **Pitch 1:** Climb a slab and pass the roof on its left side. Belay at a crack up left. A tree belay is higher if you have a 70-meter rope. **Pitch 2:**

First Flatiron

Climb directly up the left-facing dihedral, then work right over a bulge to *Baker's Way,* a right-traversing ramp system. Continue up a slab past a bolt and belay down right of a couple trees. **Pitch 3:** Climb to a left-facing dihedral or up a slab past a small tree and then up past some small roofs. **Pitch 4:** Move up left on a slab and pull past the long, obvious roof (5.5). Climb directly up, aiming for the left side of a left-angling hanging dihedral to a belay at a piton (if you can find it!). **Pitch 5:** Climb past the left edge of the dihedral and cruise the upper slab to a ridge belay. **Pitch 6:** Follow the ridge up left, passing a couple steps, to the summit. This can be broken into two pitches.

THIRD FLATIRON

The *East Face* of the 1,300-foot-high Third Flatiron is the most popular easy climb in Boulder and Colorado. It's easy to access, offers lots of fun climbing, has stunning views from the summit, and is simply the best beginner route anywhere. It was first climbed in 1906 by Floyd and Earl Millard. The *East Face* route has been climbed in roller skates and naked, has been soloed in less than ten minutes, and is climbed by thousands every year.

Climb the popular Third Flatiron during the week to avoid the crowds. Despite the route's easy climbing, do not take it lightly. Many accidents have occurred on it. The climb has little protection, is dangerous if wet

or snowy, is difficult to retreat from, and the rappels off the backside are difficult for beginners. Be prepared when climbing it by carrying extra clothes, snacks, and water. Also, get off the summit on summer afternoons if thunderstorms are approaching. Bring a 200-foot (60-meter) rope and a small rack with sets of Stoppers and cams to 2 inches.

The Third, as locals call it, is closed from February 1 to July 31 for nesting falcons. Check with the Boulder Open Space office at Chautauqua Park for current closures.

Finding the crag: From US 36 or South Broadway, drive west on Baseline Road toward Flagstaff Mountain. Turn left into Chautauqua Park and park in the lot. Hike south up Mesa Trail along the paved Bluebell Road (closed to traffic) to Bluebell Shelter. From the shelter, follow the Royal Arch Trail to the Third Flatiron Trail to the northeast corner of the Flatiron's east face and the start of the route.

Descent: Descend from the Third Flatiron's summit by rappelling. Three rappels with a single rope or two rappels with double ropes from fixed eyebolts lead down the steep west face. The eyebolts have attached rappel directions showing distance to the next station. **Rappel 1:** Rappel 40 feet over an overhang to the South Bowl. **Rappel 2:** Rappel 50 feet from the south edge of the bowl to Friday's Folly Ledge, a narrow, exposed ledge on a vertical face. Be sure to knot the

2 or 3 rappels
down West Face

end of your rope to ensure you do not rappel off its end. Traverse west from an eyebolt along the ledge to another eyebolt and the third rappel. **Rappel 3:** Rappel 70 feet west to the West Bench. Do not rappel from the first eyebolt on the ledge without double ropes; it's a 140-foot semi-free rappel to the ground from there. After rappelling to the base, scramble north and follow a trail down the north side of the formation back to the approach trail.

1. East Face (5.4 R) 800 feet. This excellent classic route wanders up the center of the immense 50-degree-angled face. The route follows six large belay eyebolts that were placed in 1931 for guided parties. The first and last pitches are the hardest. Begin at the end of the Third Flatiron Trail and below an arête that divides the slabby east face from the vertical

> The *East Face* of the Third Flatiron is Colorado's most famous and storied climbing route. Brothers Floyd and Earl Millard climbed it in 1906—Colorado's first technical rock climb. In the 1950s Dale Johnson made a roller-skate ascent. In the 1970s Gary Neptune climbed it in the nude, and later Malcolm Daly soloed it without using his hands.

north face. **Pitch 1:** Traverse up left past a bolt, cross a water trough, and climb a rib to an eyebolt belay. **Pitch 2:** Climb straight up to a belay stance at a flake. **Pitch 3:** Climb easy rock to an eyebolt and belay. Climbing left is 4th class, while right is 5.2. **Pitch 4:** Easy climbing (5.0) leads to a fifth eyebolt below the C on the painted CU logo. **Pitch 5:** Climb up the C on easy rock to the last eyebolt just left of the base of The Gash, a large chimney. **Pitch 6:** Climb left of The Gash up steep, easy rock for 100 feet to a belay. **Pitch 7:** Climb 100 feet to a belay atop a chockstone at the top of The Gash. **Pitch 8:** Cross The Gash and smear up Desolation Flats, a friction face with runout, easy rock, to the summit. A direct finish goes right of The Gash for two long pitches to the summit.

SATAN'S SLAB

Satan's Slab, also called Ridge Two, presents an impressive, smooth east face that dominates the north side of Skunk Canyon behind the NCAR complex. The long slab offers lots of superb but poorly protected friction climbing that is harder than that found on the First and Third Flatirons. The slab is usually closed for raptor nesting from February 1 through July 31. Check at the Ranger Cottage at Chautauqua Park for current closures.

Finding the crag: From either downtown Boulder or from the south, drive on South Broadway Street (CO 93) to a turn onto Table

Joseffa Meir dancing with the devil on *Satan's Slab* (5.8 R). PHOTO ANDREW BURR

Mesa Drive, just north of Neptune Mountaineering. Follow the road uphill to a parking area at NCAR (National Center for Atmospheric Research). Hike 0.5 mile west on NCAR Trail to Mesa Trail. Turn right (north) for about 600 feet, crossing Skunk Creek. Look for a rough path that heads west. Follow it up into Skunk Canyon, passing under Ridge One (Stairway to Heaven), a long slabby ridge with a big roof. Satan's Slab is the next big ridge on the right. Hiking time is about forty-five minutes.

Descent: Downclimb a chimney to a ledge and follow it north. Hike back down the north side to the slab base.

1. Satan's Slab (5.8 R) Excellent adventure—expect runouts on 5.5 climbing. The first two pitches are mostly unprotected. Start at the low point of the formation above Skunk Creek. Locate an obvious, big roof high above. **Pitch 1:** Begin with friction moves and then cruise an easy unprotected slab to a belay at a fixed piton about 30 feet below the roof. 200 feet. **Pitch 2:** Work up toward the left side of the roof past a couple pitons. Yard over the roof's left side (well-protected 5.8). Climb up left to a crack that leads up right to the ridge (5.7). Finish up an easy slab (5.4) to a belay left of a small roof. There are only two belay spots where you can get more than a single anchor in; look

Skunk Canyon

Ridge One

.4

.5

.7 R

.8

.7

1

carefully. **Pitch 3:** Delicate smears go left of another roof (5.7 R) to easier climbing. **Pitch 4:** Climb a flared crack on the right or scamper up easily to the left. **Pitch 5:** Continue up and join the upper ridge. Follow it easily to a rounded summit. **Pitch 6:** Climb easy rock to a headwall, which is bouldered (5.8) or passed on the right. After belaying, scramble up a couple hundred feet on easy rock to the base of the final tower. **Pitches 7 and 8:** Climb onto the east face slab and friction directly to the summit (5.4 R). Or jam a crack west of the ridge crest (5.8+) to the top.

SEAL ROCK

Seal Rock, a seal-shaped Flatiron perched high above Bear Canyon on the Nebel Horn, offers a classic route up the left side of its 850-foot-high east face. Like all the slabby Flatiron routes, it's a bit sporty with long runouts on easy climbing and offers a spectacular free rappel down the overhanging north face. This rappel, not for beginners, will air your pants out! The low-angle face offers plenty of solitude, great scenery, and lots of climbing possibilities on the hold-studded slab. Many variations are possible on this route description—your experience may be different. Bring a small rack as well as lots of slings to tie off flakes and chickenheads. Note that Seal Rock is not part of the annual raptor closure area in adjoining Fern Canyon.

Finding the crag: From US 36 in downtown Boulder, or CO 93 from the south, follow South Broadway Street to Table Mesa Drive, which is just north of Neptune Mountaineering. Turn west onto Table Mesa Drive, follow it to NCAR (National Center for Atmospheric Research), and park in the large lot. The NCAR trailhead is on the north side of the building. Hike west, following signs to Mesa Trail, for 0.5 mile. Turn left onto Mesa Trail and hike 0.5 mile downhill to Boulder Canyon Creek. Continue up the trail for another 0.3 mile to its junction with Bear Canyon Trail at a switchback.

Hike 50 yards south from the junction and look for the unmarked Harmon Cave Trail on the right. Follow this rough path up a steep slope for 0.25 mile to gated Harmon Cave. Look for a climber's path to the left before the cave and follow it uphill to the lowest corner of Seal Rock on its north side.

Leave your packs here and gear up so after descending you don't have to reclimb the hill to the route's start. Continue up the steep hill on the outside of The Pup, a flatironette at the base of Seal Rock, to the southeast corner of the rock. The route begins at the juncture of the east and south faces below a deep crack. Allow 1.5 hours to hike from parking lot to cliff.

Descent: Downclimb back to the chains at the top of pitch 5. Rappel 185 feet with double ropes down the overhanging north face—one of

Seal Rock

Boulder's most spectacular rappels! Most of the rappel is free. Use caution and a fireman's belay at the base. Not for beginners.

1. East Face Left (5.5 R) Start below an obvious tree and a deep crack on the southeast corner of the east face. The crack separates the main slab from The Pup. **Pitch 1:** Climb the slab just left of the crack (5.5 R) for 30 feet, then head directly up the unprotected slab to easier terrain. Belay at the tree on a good ledge.

Pitch 2: Climb a jug ladder directly above the tree or traverse left to a shallow groove. Either way, climb fun rock (5.2) to a belay stance at a large flake. **Pitch 3:** Climb up left past a big chickenhead, then up right on juggy rock (5.3) to a belay on ledges below the steeper upper wall split by a crack. Or climb directly up from the belay on easy unprotected rock (5.3) to the belay. **Pitch 4:** Climb big flakes and then cruise an excellent pro-eating finger crack (5.4) to a belay stance. **Pitch 5:** Scramble up easy rock (4th class) to a 2-bolt rappel anchor with chains on the edge of the north face. Belay here, then scramble 25 feet to the summit and admire the fabulous view and potholes teeming with fairy shrimp. **Rack:** Medium to large Stoppers, cams to 3 inches, 6 to 8 slings, two 200-foot (60-meter) ropes.

THE FATIRON

The Fatiron is a 1,100-foot-high Flatiron immediately north of The Maiden. The slab divides into three sections. The lowest is The Fatironette, a 100-foot broken slab below the main face. The middle is a long, narrow 700-foot slab that ends atop an airy summit. Below it to the west is a deep notch that separates this summit from the 350-foot upper slab and the highest summit. The formation is outside the closed raptor nesting area in Shadow Canyon.

The long *East Face* route is an easy climb with only a few sections of harder climbing. Gerry Roach, in his *Flatiron Classics* book, calls the route one of the ten best Flatiron climbs. The views of The Maiden are spectacular from the route. Like most Flatiron climbs, protection is sometimes tricky but you can climb almost anywhere. This is an adventure route with sections of downclimbing and a rappel into the notch. Allow plenty of time to approach the formation, climb the route, and do the boulder-hopping descent down the gully to the north.

This description adds a starting warm-up pitch on The Fatironette.

Finding the crag: Park at the South Mesa trailhead parking area off CO 170 south of Boulder and before Eldorado Springs. Hike northwest on Mesa Trail until you are east of The Maiden and The Fatiron. Locate an old stone water tank on the east side of the trail at the junction of Mesa Trail and Shadow Canyon Trail. Walk left (south) on Shadow Canyon Trail for a few hundred feet to a path that scrambles up past an old quarry, then head north on a wide, level stone path for a hundred yards. Look for a climber's path that heads up left through trees between two talus fields. Hike up the steep path to a faint path that goes right (north) and climbs a boulder field to the base of The Fatironette, the lowest slab. Alternatively, hike around the north side of the slab and scramble up easy rock to a saddle between The Fatironette and the main slab. Don't go too far up the trail to The Maiden or you will have to backtrack and reclimb up to The Fatiron since the route cannot be accessed from the south. If you miss the trails to the area, follow your nose and hike uphill, and you will eventually find the trails. Allow 1.5 to 2 hours from car to cliff. Be prepared to get lost.

Descent: Downclimb 10 feet from the summit to a tree with rappel slings. Rappel 50 feet to the base. Descend a talus field on the north side of The Fatiron, then work right to the base of The Fatironette.

1. East Face (5.6 R) Lots of belay stances are available so pitches can be strung differently than described. Much of the route is easily simul-climbed. Begin below The Fatironette, a broken slab. **Pitch 1:** Climb an easy slab (4th class) for 100 feet and belay on top. **Pitch 2:** Downclimb west over the highest hump (3rd class) and scramble to a belay at a tree in a hole.

Pitch 3: Climb easy rock (3rd class), pass a big tree, and belay on a small ledge below the main slab. **Pitch 4:** Follow a thin crack system (5.6) past three small trees to a flake belay stance on the left. 140 feet. Climbing is harder left of the crack and easier to the right. **Pitch 5:** Continue up the crack system to a headwall with a crack (5.4). Belay on a shelf above or on a higher ledge. 150 feet. **Pitch 6:** Easy climbing leads up a crack and juggy headwall (5.3) to a belay from a tied-off arch on the first summit. 200 feet. **Pitch 7:** Downclimb west on easy rock (3rd class) for 100 feet to a tree with rappel slings. Rappel 50 feet to a big tree. Scramble up right to a belay ledge (no anchors) below the final slab. **Pitch 8:** Climb directly up the slab (5.2) to the top of a pillar and belay. 150 feet. **Pitch 9:** Smear straight up from the stance (5.6 R) for 50 feet to a bushy tree. Climb up left (5.4) past bigger trees to The Fatiron summit. 200 feet. Alternatively, climb the face to the left or right of the described way, but expect scant pro down low. **Rack:** Sets of Stoppers and TCUs; Camalots to #2; 6 to 8 runners; 200-foot (60-meter) rope.

The Fatiron

The descent off The Maiden is one of the most spectacular free rappels in Colorado.
PHOTO ANDREW BURR

THE MAIDEN

The Maiden, a towering sandstone pinnacle perched on a narrow ridge, is not only the most spectacular Flatiron summit but it's also the toughest and scariest. The best climb is the historic *North Face* route, which traverses across an airy ridge to the peak's sheer North Face to a final easy slab. Descent from the summit is by a photogenic 110-foot free rappel down the overhanging West Face. Expect solitude, scenic views, and great climbing on The Maiden. Bring a standard Flatirons rack with a set of Stoppers and cams to 3 inches. Lots of fixed pitons are found on the route.

Finding the crag: Park at the South Mesa trailhead parking area off CO 170 south of Boulder and before Eldorado Springs. Hike northwest on Mesa Trail until you are east of The Maiden and The Fatiron. Locate an old stone water tank on the east side of the trail at the junction of Mesa Trail and Shadow Canyon Trail. Walk left (south) on Shadow Canyon Trail for a few hundred feet to a path that scrambles up past an old quarry, then head north on a wide, level stone path for a hundred yards. Look for a climber's path that heads up left through trees between two talus fields. Hike up the steep path to the base of The Maiden's East Ridge. To reach the *North Face* and *West Overhang* routes, continue up a steep path on either the north or south side of the formation (south if you're planning on leaving packs at the base of the rappels). Watch for poison ivy and rattlesnakes in summer. Allow 1.5 to 2 hours from car to crag for the 3-mile hike.

Descent: Rappel 110 feet with double ropes from anchors above the *West Overhang*. This free rappel lands at the Crow's Nest. Scramble west along the ridge to a downclimb or make another double-rope 120-foot rappel from an eyebolt down the south face of the ridge. The landing at the Crow's Nest is scary in wind. Tie knots in the ends of your ropes. Rappel with a 200-foot (60-meter) cord but make sure it is full length because

you won't have much left. Better to use a 70-meter rope.

1. North Face (5.6 R) Excellent, classic, exposed, and interesting. Lots of traversing and downclimbing—carry slings for prussiks. A fall could strand a climber on the wall. Belay beginners from both sides. Leave packs below the face south of the Crow's Nest and scramble up boulders to the west end of The Maiden fin. **Pitch 1:** Climb a 40-foot, west-facing wall (5.4 R) to a summit and view of The Maiden. **Pitch 2:** Downclimb easy slabs on the narrow ridge (5.3) to the Crow's Nest notch and a belay/rappel eyebolt. The leader, on toprope, should place pro

The Maiden

The exposed 110-foot free rappel off The Maiden is Colorado's most famous and most photographed rappel. Brad Van Diver made the first descent of this spectacular and scary rappel in 1952.

for the second. **Pitch 3:** Downclimb a ramp on the north face for 35 feet, then climb up left on good holds on a steep, exposed face (5.6 R) to a belay ledge with a tree. Alternatively, climb the short face directly up (5.7) to a fixed piton and then left to the tree. This pitch can be protected by scrambling east from the Crow's Nest and clipping an old piton. **Pitch 4:** Tricky climbing with lots of variations, minimal gear, and rope drag. Climb up left from the tree to a short corner to a ramp ledge. Climb down east on the exposed ramp to the base of a crack in a right-facing corner. Traverse left around the corner's edge and climb an exposed narrow ramp up left to a belay ledge in an alcove. The vertical crack can be climbed direct (5.7) or do *The Walton Traverse* (5.5)—climb up left from the tree to a vertical face. Pass two old bolts and then traverse up left to a piton in a right-facing corner (5.5 R). Continue up left to the alcove belay. **Pitch 5:** Climb the steep face above the belay (5.4) and then the upper East Ridge (5.4) to the amazing summit.

2. West Overhang (5.11b) Classic Boulder route. Use double ropes if you do it in one pitch. Second should be competent to avoid epics. Use lots of slings to avoid rope drag. Begin at the west end of The Maiden's long ridge (same start as *North Face*). **Pitch 1:** Climb a 40-foot, west-facing wall (5.4 R) to a summit. **Pitch 2:** Downclimb easy slabs on the ridge (5.3) to the Crow's Nest notch and a belay/rappel eyebolt. **Pitch 3:** Climb slabby rock to the base of the vertical wall. Climb a thin crack (5.9) right of the left arête to a small stance below the leaning roof. Continue straight up and around the left edge of a big roof (5.8) to an obvious traverse. Climb right 15 feet (5.8) to the base of a slot. Thrutch up the slot (5.11a/b) to the summit.

THE MATRON

The Matron, a Maiden clone, lifts its narrow profile above Shadow Canyon on the east side of South Boulder Peak's long south ridge. The formation, resembling a clenched fist, offers a slabby east ridge flanked by vertical north and south faces. The moderate *East Ridge* and *North Face* routes are worthy climbs that reach The Matron's spectacular summit. Unfortunately the crag is usually closed from February 1 through July 31 for nesting raptors, so time your visit accordingly. Check with Boulder Mountain Parks for closure updates. Bring a standard rack with sets of Stoppers and cams to 3 inches.

The Matron

2 rappels
down West Face

2 climb 2 pitches
up
North Face

1

Finding the crag: Park at the South Mesa trailhead parking area off CO 170 south of Boulder and just before Eldorado Springs. Follow the Mesa Trail for about 1.5 miles to the Shadow Canyon Trail. Hike up Shadow Canyon Trail until The Matron is obvious above you. Locate a climber's path that heads up left. Follow it to the base of the East Ridge and then right to the north side of The Matron. Hiking distance is 2.3 miles. Allow an hour to approach.

Descent: Two rappels. Locate an eyebolt on the west side of the summit. Rappel 80 feet west to a pair of eyebolts at a stance below an overhanging section on the right side of the west face. Rappel 100 feet west to a notch below the west face. Hike down a climber's path on the north side of The Matron.

1. East Ridge (5.5 R) Classic, fun, and easy. A large overhang blocks access to the ridge below its toe. Start 50 feet right of the toe below a slab at the edge of the north face (right of overhang). **Pitch 1:** Edge up the unprotected slab (5.5 R) to a shelf and then follow an awkward crack (5.5 crux) up left to a ledge. Step left to a flake and pull over a roof above to the low-angle East Ridge. Continue to a belay at a flake. **Pitch 2:** Fun moves up the right side of the narrow edge (5.4 R) lead to a good belay ledge above the north face. **Pitch 3:** Continue up the steeper ridge above (5.4) to a belay ledge. **Pitch 4:** Climb featured rock (5.4) to a belay ledge or continue up a short headwall to the summit with a long rope.

2. North Face (5.6) Excellent historic climb. Pitches can be combined. To find the start from the toe of the East Ridge, scramble along the north side for 200 feet, then climb a short chimney formed by a slabby block to a good ledge below a couple crack systems. **Pitch 1:** Climb a steep, left-angling crack system to a prominent roof. Jam and layback over it (5.6) to a tree belay. **Pitch 2:** Continue up the steep crack system above (5.6) to the East Ridge and belay up right on a good ledge. **Pitch 3:** Climb the steeper ridge above (5.4) to a good ledge belay. **Pitch 4:** Finish up the long slabby ridge (5.4) to an obvious ledge belay or continue up a headwall to the summit with a long rope.

Flagstaff Mountain

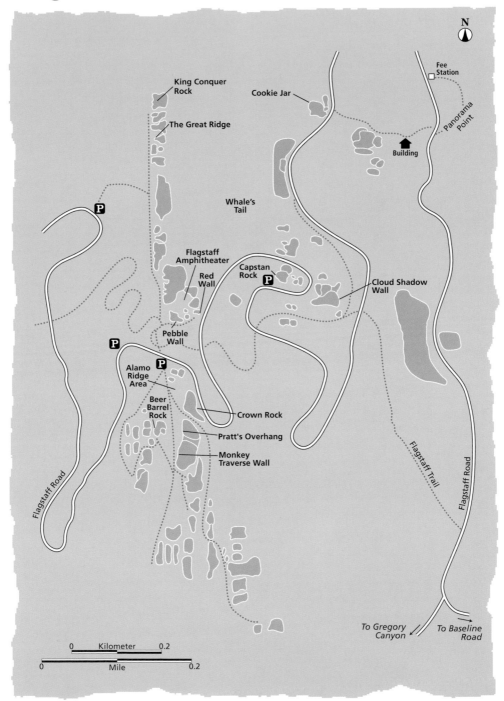

N

King Conquer Rock

The Great Ridge

Cookie Jar

Fee Station

Panorama Point

Building

Whale's Tail

P

Flagstaff Amphitheater

Red Wall

Capstan Rock

P

Cloud Shadow Wall

Pebble Wall

P

Alamo Ridge Area

P

Beer Barrel Rock

Crown Rock

Pratt's Overhang

Monkey Traverse Wall

Flagstaff Road

Flagstaff Trail

Flagstaff Road

To Gregory Canyon

To Baseline Road

| 0 | Kilometer | 0.2 |
| 0 | Mile | 0.2 |

4.

Flagstaff Mountain Bouldering

Flagstaff Mountain, with its easy access from Boulder, is Colorado's historic bouldering area. Numerous boulders, with a wide variety of problems and difficulties, scatter across the upper flanks of 6,872-foot Flagstaff Mountain, forming a playground for both the beginner and expert boulderer. The boulders, composed of coarse conglomerate sandstone, offer lots of moves with pebble-pinches, shallow sloped dishes, sharp flakes, finger pockets, and gritty edges. The granular rock quickly shreds fingertips, especially after multiple attempts on a problem.

Use care when bouldering on Flagstaff. While most of the problems have good landings, some do not. Utilize a spotter and a crash pad to avoid twisted or broken ankles. Use chalk sparingly and brush the holds before you leave.

Flagstaff Mountain is in Boulder Mountain Park, a large open space parkland that preserves Boulder's mountain skyline. Residents can use the park for free. Visitors must purchase a daily park pass at a kiosk at Panorama Point a half mile up the road or at Crown Rock parking area and display the pass in the vehicle window.

Flagstaff offers bouldering year-round. The best seasons, as elsewhere in Colorado, are spring and fall. Spring days can be variable in temperature but precipitation is usually light. It can be windy. Fall is perfect with lots of clear, warm days. Summers are good but can be hot. Climb in the evening and morning for the best conditions. The boulders are accessible all winter, although snow lingers below the north-facing boulders.

Getting there: Flagstaff Mountain is easily reached from Boulder via

Pat Ament did the first ascents of many classic boulder problems on Flagstaff in the 1960s. Bouldering, of course, wasn't a popular pursuit then but a way to practice hard moves. Pat says he was usually the only climber up there. "No one else would know or comprehend what I had done or was doing."

Baseline Road. From Denver, exit US 36 onto Baseline Road. From downtown Boulder, drive south on North Broadway Street to Baseline Road at the southern edge of the University of Colorado campus. Drive west on Baseline Road through a residential area to Flagstaff Mountain. All mileages begin from Armstrong Bridge, a small bridge at the mountain base. Baseline Road turns into Flagstaff Road here. Purchase a daily park pass, unless you're a Boulder County resident, at the Panorama Point kiosk. The curvy road quickly climbs the mountain. The best boulders are near the mountain crest. Park well off the road at designated pull-offs and watch for bicyclists on the road.

PANORAMA POINT AREA
Cookie Jar

The 25-foot-high Cookie Jar is one of Flagstaff's classic boulders but isn't as popular as it was in the 1960s. The problems are all pretty high. Unless you're sure of yourself, use a toprope for safety. Use an eyebolt and gear on top for an anchor. The roadside block has lots of great history. *Northcutt's Roll,* an old problem, was first done by hardman Ray Northcutt in the 1950s. On one attempt, he fell off the boulder and rolled down to the road.

Finding the boulder: The boulder is on the west side of the road at 0.8 mile from Armstrong Bridge. Park down the road from the boulder at the Flagstaff House parking area at

The first time Pat Ament saw *Northcutt's Roll* climbed was in the 1960s when Bob Culp, who worked at the climbing shop Holubar, picked Pat up after work and went to the Cookie Jar. Bob, dressed in a suit and tie, took off his jacket and put on his Kronhoeffer rock shoes and proceeded to crank the problem—in shirt and tie!

0.7 mile. Walk up the road's shoulder to the boulder. Problems start at the corner above the road.

Descent: Downclimb the west side of the boulder.

1. Northcutt's Roll (V3) Overhanging wall on the southeast corner above the road.

2. Right Shield (V1) Start 6 feet right of *Cookie Jar Crack.* Grab good edges up the bulging face.

3. Left Shield (V1) Just right of the crack. Pull edges up the face.

4. Cookie Jar Crack (V0-/5.7) Excellent and fun problem up the obvious crack on the south face. Popular as a beginner toprope.

5. Russian's Nose (V1) Exposed highball. Climb the overhang left of *Cookie Jar Crack.*

Cookie Jar

6. Commitment (V4) No topo. Pat Ament 1964 problem. Climb a committing bulge on the right side of the north face. Bad landing.

7. Jackson's Pitch (V2) No topo. On the north face. Reach over a bulge from an undercling left of *Commitment.*

Capstan Rock

Capstan Rock, a large obvious pillar, is an excellent roadside boulder on a hairpin turn. The south and west faces offer the longest and best problems. The 35-foot-high boulder has lots of highballs. Use pads or sling a couple horns on top for a toprope anchor. Keep off the road and watch out for passing gawkers.

Finding the boulder: Drive up the road for 1.5 miles to a sharp hairpin turn and park in a small pullout.

Descent: To descend from the top, downclimb the north face. From the top of the flake atop *South Crack,* continue to the top or downclimb to the right and jump off or do tricky moves on the boulder to the east.

1. West Face (V1 X) Fun highball. Climb shallow huecos and pockets on the boulder's west side. It's scary up high; don't fall or use a rope.

2. Sarabande (V2 X) Start up just left of *South Crack,* using edges and pockets up the steep face.

3. South Crack (V2 X) Jam piton scars up the obvious crack that slices across Capstan's south face. Start is the crux.

4. South Overhang (V4) Climb the slight bulge just right of *South Crack* on slopers and pebbles. Finish up the crack.

5. Just Right (V7) Desperate Jim Holloway problem. Tackle the overhang right of *South Overhang* with sloping holds, laybacks, and delicate friction moves. Crux is a lunge to a pocket. It's V10 if you don't use a cheater stone.

Cloud Shadow Wall

Cloud Shadow Wall, a large boulder pile north of the road, is one of Flagstaff's premiere bouldering spots with lots of great problems. An adjacent boulder, The Alcove, offers more classics. Lots of problems and variations exist on this long south-facing wall. It's often crowded on nice days with its sunny exposure and moderate problems.

Finding the boulder: Cloud Shadow is immediately east of Capstan Rock and the hairpin turn. Drive 1.5 miles up the road and park at a pullout by Capstan. Walk east on the road to the right side of the hairpin turn, step over the guardrail, and follow a short trail down right to the south side of Cloud Shadow. The boulder is just east of the turn.

Descent: Downclimb the slabby east side of the boulder.

Capstan Rock

downclimb north face

downclimb
down right

1

2

3

4

5

Tommy Caldwell cranks the classic problem *Hagan's Wall* on Cloud Shadow Boulder, Flagstaff Mountain.

1. Dandy Line (V6) Left of *Hagan's Wall* is a pebble-pulling route. The starting edge is slowly crumbling away.

2. Hagan's Wall (V5) Excellent classic problem—one of Flag's best. Climbs a steep bulge on the left side of the long wall. Start with a painful flake and shallow two-finger pocket and throw the right hand to a rail. Dyno to pebbles and climb up right to easier rock.

Cloud Shadow Wall

Upper
Traverse V1

Lower Traverse V4

2

3

4

3. Cloud Shadow Traverse Upper and Lower (V1 and V4 respectively) An upper and lower traverse swings across a band of pockets and sloping ramps on the south face. Good training problem with lots of variations. The lower traverse is harder than the higher pocketed traverse (V1). Start in the middle of the wall at the first handrail. Traverse left and finish up a tricky ramp and face. Harder traverses begin on the far right side of the boulder.

4. Contemplation (V1) On the right side of the wall. Grab some pockets and climb along a left-leaning seam to a scary headwall.

5. Moderate Bulge (V0) Good problem. Same start as *Contemplation* but move up right to a hole. Undercling and grab edges on a shelf. Finish up right.

6. The Consideration (V4) One of Flagstaff's best problems. Begin at an

Jim Holloway, who grew up in Boulder, did a lot of hard problems on Flagstaff. *Trice,* his toughest one, was probably the hardest boulder problem in the world when it was done in 1975. It was unrepeated until 2007.

Cloud Shadow Wall

obvious hole. Work up right to a sloping edge; finish with a committing throw up right to a rail.

7. Trice aka A.H.R. (Another Holloway Route) (V12) Visionary Holloway problem from 1975. A hard sequence up minute edges and pebbles—a very specific set of holds.

8. Bob's Bulge (V5) Far right side of the wall. Begin by grabbing holds under the bulge. Work up with hand slaps and heel and toe hooks to the ridge above.

9. East Inside Corner (V1) Climbs a short corner just right of the southeast corner. Pull into the corner, stand up, and move delicately up the slab above.

A few superb problems are at The Alcove. Walk west from *Hagan's Wall* around a corner of the boulder to an alcove gap.

The Alcove

10. East Overhang Crack (V2) Good problem. Climb a crack before the alcove to a difficult mantle over a prominent roof.

11. Sailor's Delight (V1) Excellent! Swing up and over a bulging roof above The Alcove with cut-loose jugs at the lip.

ALAMO RIDGE AREA

Some of Flagstaff Mountain's best classic problems lie north and south of the road along the west side of Alamo Ridge, a long, tilted sandstone ridge that runs north–south down the mountainside.

Finding the area: Drive up the road for 2 miles from Armstrong Bridge and park in the Crown Rock parking area on the south side of the road. A parking pay station is at the lot. The small parking lot is often full since the area is not only popular with climbers but also with hikers and picnickers. More parking is up the road. Unless you are a Boulder County resident, you must display a parking pass, which you can buy at the lot.

Crown Rock

Crown Rock sits southeast of the lot alongside the road. This low-angle Flatiron offers many good beginner topropes on its east, south, and west faces.

Pratt's Overhang

Follow a trail about 150 feet south of the parking area to Pratt's Overhang, a well-traveled, west-facing overhang

> The famous Yosemite climber and off-width crack master Chuck Pratt never climbed *Pratt's Overhang.* The route was named for him because Chuck had a reputation for pressing difficult mantles on boulders around Camp 4 in Yosemite Valley.

on the path. Some great classic problems edge up this boulder, including *Pratt's Overhang,* which Bob Culp first climbed in 1960.

Descent: Scramble off the backside.

1. Pratt's Mantle (V2) Do an obvious awkward mantle on the left-side bulge.

Pratt's Overhang

2. Pratt's Overhang (V2) Climb the right-leaning shallow crack/slot.

3. Smith Overhang (V8) Pull the overhanging wall right of the slot using sharp edges.

4. Crystal Corner (V2) Climb the steep, blunt arête on the right with a large crystal.

Monkey Traverse

Just down the trail from Pratt's Overhang is the Monkey Traverse wall, featuring *Monkey Traverse,* probably Flagstaff's most frequented problem. This popular pump follows the obvious chalked holds across the wall and offers many variations and eliminates.

A few other dyno and roof problems bisect the traverse.

Descent: Scramble off the backside.

1. Monkey Traverse (V4) Excellent. One of Flagstaff's best and most popular problems. The traverse is usually done right to left. Bonus points for doing it both ways.

2. West Overhang (V1 X) Locate this highball classic in the middle of the traverse. Climb to a rest below the roof, crimp an edge, and make a long reach to a jug. Pull over the big overhang.

Monkey Traverse

Beer Barrel Rock

Beer Barrel Rock

Beer Barrel Rock is a great boulder with a dozen fun problems on its slabby east face and overhanging west face. From *Monkey Traverse,* hike west on a trail to the boulder.

    Descent: Downclimb the *East Slab* route.

1. East Slab (V0) No topo. Great beginner problem and standard downclimb route.

2. Poling Pebble Route (V5) Poling's pebble pulled out, so grab edges and crystals up the southeast corner.

3. South Face (V0) Fun moves on edges to a final reach.

4. Southwest Corner (V0) One of Flag's finest problems. Climb layback flakes up the steep face on the right side of *West Traverse.*

5. Hritz Overhang (V3) Left of *Southwest Corner.* Pull up on pockets and pebbles.

6. West Traverse (V3) Pumpy traverse across the boulder's steep west face.

FLAGSTAFF AMPHITHEATER AREA

The area north of the main parking area above Alamo Ridge offers a splendid assortment of boulders and problems, including lots of fun classics.

Finding the boulders: To find the area, drive up the road for 2 miles from Armstrong Bridge and park and pay (nonresident fee, if necessary) at the Crown Rock parking lot on the south side of the road. If this lot is full, park farther up the road. Cross the road and hike north on the Flagstaff Trail to a junction 200 feet from the road. Take the right fork to the first boulder, the Pebble Wall, which is 300 feet from the road and partially hidden by pine trees. For other boulders, continue hiking past Pebble Wall to North Rocks and then up right to Red Wall. Continue uphill to the west to Flagstaff Amphitheater.

Pebble Wall

The Pebble Wall, shaded by pine trees, is the first boulder encountered north of the road. This excellent boulder offers some of Flagstaff's classic hard problems on its bulging and pebble-covered south face.

Descent: Downclimb the backside of the boulder.

Pebble Wall

The first time John Gill visited Flagstaff, he refused to climb some problems because he was afraid the crystals and knobs would break when he weighted them. Pat Ament assured him they were solid and rarely broke. John then yanked on a solid baseball-sized crystal which promptly pulled out. John laughed and told Pat, "So they never pull out, eh?"

1. Original Route (V0) High step over the bulge, then grab good pebbles to a two-handed undercling on a flake.

2. Crystal Mantle (V2) Mantle onto a large crystal and climb up right.

3. Direct South Face (V2) Start at a tree root. Pinch pebbles and crystals to the rounded summit.

4. High Step (V1) Begin with a high step over the bulge, then crank a pebbled face.

5. South Face (V3) Thin feet, pebble pinches, high, and committing.

6. Southwest Corner (V1) A superb and airy layback problem up a rounded arête.

7. West Overhang (V3) No topo. Start left of the rounded arête on the northwest face. More tricky pebble moves to a dicey top-out. Use pads.

8. North Overhang (V0) No topo. Climb up left from *West Overhang's* start to good holds.

Red Wall

The Red Wall is simply one of Flagstaff Mountain's best boulders. Handholds, including edges, pockets, crystals, and buckets, cover its vertical south face and offer lots of great problems and many variations.

Finding the boulder: From the Crown Rock parking area, cross the road and hike up the Flagstaff Mountain Trail for a few hundred feet to Pebble Wall. Keep right, passing Pebble Wall, to the obvious Red Wall boulder.

Descent: Downclimb the backside.

Red Wall

1. Center Left (V3) On the left side of the face. Grab two jugs, heel hook, and make a long reach to a three-finger pocket. Stand up and grab crystals.

2. Standard Route (V4) Start on good holds, then step up and reach a three-finger pocket. Above, pinch a potato flake and pull onto the top.

3. Varney Direct (V5) Begin with two high handholds. Crimp thin edges to the potato chip and top out.

4. Red Wall Right Side (V5) Ultra-classic Pat Ament problem. Start left of a pine tree with your left hand in the soap dish starting hold and your right in a shallow two-finger hold. Climb to a pinch and good pocket.

The Amphitheater

The Amphitheater, immediately north of the Pebble Wall, are a couple south-facing boulders that form an amphi-theater. Many fine problems, mostly moderates, ascend these boulders. Some are high, so it's a good idea to have a crash pad and competent spotter.

Finding the boulder: From the Crown Rock parking area, hike north up the Flagstaff Mountain Trail,

The Amphitheater—Left Side

keeping right toward the Pebble Wall. Stay left of the wall and hike uphill to the boulder jumble.

Descent: Downclimb the backside of both Amphitheater boulders.

The Amphitheater—Left Side

1. Mongolian Cosmonaut (V8) No topo. A difficult and steep problem over a big bulge on the far left side. Crank pebbles and rounded edges over the fierce bulge. Some of the holds are eroding away.

2. Southwest Corner (V0) No topo. Start off a boulder. Thrutch up and over the rounded bulge.

3. High Overhang (V0) An overhang with a scary finishing mantle.

4. South Face Left (V4) Hard pulls onto a prow, then work up right to a finishing slab. Bad landing.

5. Briggs Route (V3) Start off a flat boulder and move up left in a short corner. Finish with a slab.

6. Direct South Face (V4) From the flat boulder, grab cobbles up right.

7. Crystal Swing (V2) Just left of the crack. Crux is a swinging move between crystal cobbles.

The Amphitheater—Right Side

8. Far Left (aka Career Ender) (V4) Climb up right to a tricky lip encounter.

9. Overhanging Hand Traverse (V1) Super classic and fun. Pull up right on good holds to jugs at the lip. Finish up a slab.

10. Gill Direct (V4) John Gill classic. Thin edges to a trademark Gill dyno to the final jugs.

11. Direct Route (aka Sandpaper Ledge) (V3) On the right side. Pebbles and edges to a sandpaper hold. Mantle onto the upper slab.

12. South Bulge (V1) No topo. Climb up right and around a prow.

Farther up the hill from The Amphitheater are more boulders, including The Overhang Wall with steep problems, The Great Ridge with both traversing and up problems, and King Conquer Rock. King Conquer Rock, with its severely overhanging west face, offers *King Conquer Overhang* (V3), a spectacular Pat Ament problem up a crack that splits the boulder.

River Wall

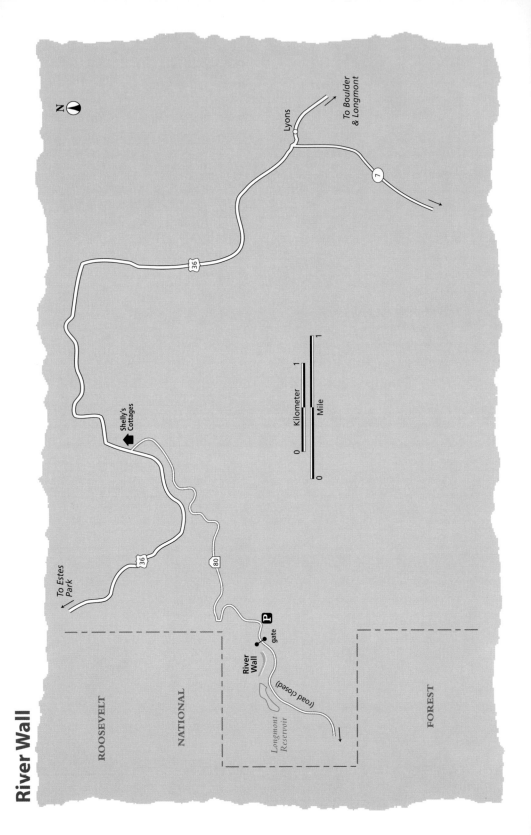

N

To Boulder
& Longmont

Lyons

7

36

To Estes
Park

Shelly's
Cottages

36

80

Kilometer

Mile

P

gate

River
Wall

(road closed)

ROOSEVELT

NATIONAL

Longmont
Reservoir

FOREST

5.

River Wall

The River Wall is a small but excellent granite outcrop along the North St. Vrain River northwest of Boulder. The compact 80-foot-high cliff, sometimes called "the best little crag in Colorado," offers a surprising number of superb routes. Expect fractured overhanging walls, steep slabs, finger cracks, sharp edges, and arm-pumping jug haul routes. The routes are divided between bolt-protected sport climbs and trad routes that require competence at placing gear.

You can climb here year-round. The west-facing crag is shaded on summer mornings. Autumn is perfect for climbing. The river runs high in late spring and early summer. Winter afternoons are often warm enough for climbing, too.

The crag, lying only 300 feet from the parking area, is easily accessed.

Follow a trail along the river's bank and then rock-hop across to the cliff base. When the river runs high, cross farther downstream and scramble up a gully east of the wall, then walk along the cliff top to fixed rappel anchors on the west side, which allow access to the cliff base.

Getting there: The River Wall hides in the mountains northwest of Boulder. Drive north from Boulder on US 36 to Lyons. Turn northwest in Lyons on US 36 toward Estes Park. Turn left (south) onto a dirt road, County Road 80, at Shelly's Cottages, 3.7 miles from Lyons. Follow the road west along the North St. Vrain River for 2.3 miles to a steel gate. Park off CR 80 and walk up the road for 100 yards. The River Wall sits on the river's north bank below the road.

belay bolt

1. Neurosurgeon (5.12a R) A great finger crack but a serious lead. Jam a thin crack over a roof and then face climb when the crack ends. Traverse up right onto a prow and finish with poorly protected moves (5.9 R) on an arête. **Rack:** Stoppers, double sets of TCUs, and Friends to #2.5.

2. Le Diamant E'ternal (5.13b) Excellent and sustained face right of a chimney. Climb a slab, then work up an arching seam with thin moves to the sixth bolt and a rest. Finish with crimps and underclings. 8 bolts to 2-bolt anchor.

3. The Box (5.7) Stem and climb up the gaping chimney. Watch for loose rock and don't belay below the leader. End at anchors on the left.

4. Introducing Meteor Dad (5.10d) Excellent technical climbing. Work up a steep slab using incut holds and tricky feet. The crux is an awkward mantle halfway up. 7 bolts to 2-bolt anchor.

5. Live Wire (5.10d) An arête to a crack to a final face. 6 bolts to 2-bolt anchor on *Meteor Dad.*

6. Escape from Alcatraz (5.11b) Difficult to access in high water. Belay from a bolt on a pedestal. Interesting and tricky up a steep slab using sidepulls and underclings. 5 bolts to 2-bolt anchor.

7. Redneck Hero (5.12a) Classic, powerful, and fun. Belay at a bolt on a pedestal (same start as *Escape from Alcatraz*). Traverse left above the water to an overhang. Climb steep, pumpy rock to a high crux. 6 bolts to 2-bolt anchor.

River Wall

8. Big, Big Monkey Man (5.12b) Approach the base from the left. Climb a crack (*Pocket Hercules*) for 30 feet to a bolt. Swing up right on buckets over steep overlaps and flakes. 5 bolts to 2-bolt anchor. **Rack:** Several #1.5 Friends.

9. Pocket Hercules (5.12a) Excellent crack over a series of small roofs with thin hand jams and fingerlocks. Occasional incut face holds offer relief. At the top, traverse right to *Monkey Man*'s anchors. **Rack:** Small to medium Friends including three #1.5s.

10. Big, Big Gunky Man (5.12a R) Scary and tricky climbing. Begin from a ledge left of *Pocket Hercules*. Climb

blocky rock over a roof, then climb past two bolts that protect hard face moves.

11. Brother from Another Planet (5.13b) Start off a ramp. Pull on unrelenting slopers and edges up an overhanging wall. 6 bolts to slings on a block.

12. Lost Horizon (5.14a) Face climb up an obvious overhanging crack on the overhanging wall.

13. New Horizon (5.12d) Perfect overhanging arête. Difficult laybacks and sidepulls lead up left. Step right from the second bolt, then move back left onto the arête at the third bolt. 5 bolts to 1-eyebolt anchor.

Ian Spencer-Green
pulls down on the
overhanging prow of
New Horizon (5.12d).

Denver Area

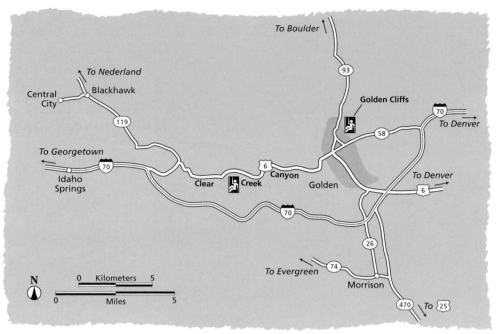

Denver rock climbers have lots of other areas to practice their vertical craft. These include the bouldering at Morrison; the granite Apron slabs and world-class bouldering on 14,264-foot Mount Evans; the short cliffs at Castlewood Canyon State Park; and the huge granite domes and walls in the South Platte region. Check out FalconGuides' *Rock Climbing Colorado* and *Bouldering Colorado* for all the beta on these great Denver climbing areas. See you on the rocks!

Denver Area

Denver, a huge sprawling city, spreads against the Front Range mountain escarpment like a sea of suburbs lapping on a rocky shore. Denver is one of the few major American cities that yields world-class climbing literally just outside the back door. The Golden Cliffs perch above the picturesque town of Golden, home to the American Alpine Club and Coors Brewery, on the south flank of North Table Mountain. This long band of volcanic basalt cliffs form a great training ground for local climbers and, best of all, they're climbable year-round. West of Golden stretches Clear Creek Canyon, a rough and ragged defile lined with vertical and overhanging crags. Clear Creek offers hundreds of bolt-protected routes that range from easy fifth-class romps to way-steep 5.14 testpieces, giving every climber an excuse to not only improve his skills but to have more fun on Denver's best climbs.

Bullet the Brown Cloud follows a perfect arête at the Brown Cloud Crags sector.

Golden Cliffs

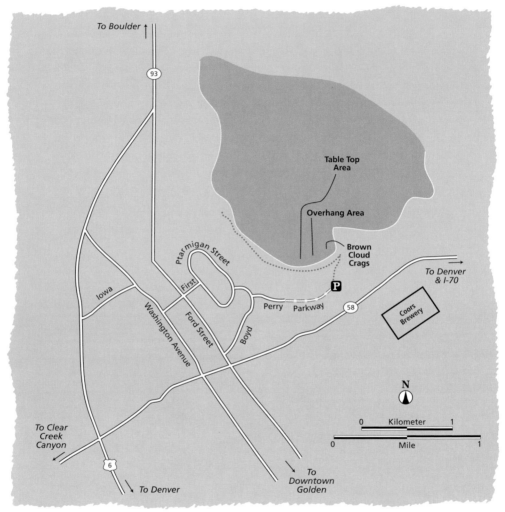

6.

Golden Cliffs

The Golden Cliffs, rising above the town of Golden on the south slope of North Table Mountain, is the most popular climbing area near Denver. It's easily accessible, offers good climbing weather with its south-facing exposure, and has lots of fun moderate routes from 40 to 60 feet long on fine compact basalt. Most of the routes are bolted sport climbs, so all you need for a day's climbing is a rope and a dozen quickdraws. Some of the crack routes, however, are also good but require a rack of gear. The Golden Cliffs are a popular toprop-ing venue, but it can be difficult to rig anchors from the top. It's better to first lead the route you want to toprope. If you are on the cliff top, use caution and don't knock any rocks off since climbers are below on the cliff-base trail. Also watch out for rattle-snakes on the trail and below climbs.

The Golden Cliffs face south and southwest and are climbable year-round. Summers can be very hot; come in the morning or evening for best temperatures. Autumn and spring days are great. It can be windy in spring. The crag shines in the win-ter with its sunny exposure, and any snow quickly melts away.

Getting there: From Denver and I-25, drive west on I-70 to CO 58 (which joins US 6 and continues west from Golden up Clear Creek Canyon). Exit onto Washington Avenue. Drive north on Washington to First Street. Turn right and follow First Street to Ptarmigan Street, which turns into Perry Parkway. Follow it to a park-ing area at the road's end and the trailhead. From Boulder, drive south on CO 93 and exit left (south) onto either Ford or Washington Streets. Drive a few blocks southeast and turn left (east) onto First Street. Fol-low to Ptarmigan Street to Perry Parkway and the parking lot.

The trail ascends steeply to the cliffs. Allow fifteen minutes of hiking time.

Climbers have the late Golden native Joseph Mayford Peery (1920–2009) to thank for preserv-ing climber access to the Golden Cliffs. Mr. Peery enjoyed seeing climbers use his land on North Table Mountain, so in 1995 he donated 28 acres to the Access Fund to allow continued use by climbers. He also donated over $20,000 for the trail and trailhead facilities. Thanks, Mr. Peery!

BROWN CLOUD CRAGS

The Brown Cloud Crags is one of the most popular sectors at Golden Cliffs. It's the first area encountered after you hike up the access trail. The sector begins on the east side of the cliffs with the first routes facing a broad gully.

Descent: Lower or rappel off fixed anchors on all routes.

Climbing is often possible along Colorado's Front Range during the winter months. Here Josh Morris tackles *Louise* (5.8), a nice moderate route on the Brown Cloud Crags.

1. Louise (5.8) No topo. Far right side. Climb a face using the right-hand arête. 3 bolts to 2-bolt anchor.

2. Thelma (5.7) No topo. Good short line on an arête facing the gully. 3 bolts to 2-bolt anchor.

3. Kid's Climb (5.9+) An east-facing route where the cliff bends into the gully. 3 bolts to 2-bolt anchor.

4. New River Gorge Homesick Blues (5.9+ R) Face climb up a narrow pillar. 3 bolts to 2-bolt anchor.

5. The Virus (5.12a) Crank a roof, then climb up left. 4 bolts to 2-bolt anchor.

6. Unnamed (5.10c/d) Climb the right side of a panel. 4 bolts to 2-bolt anchor.

7. Big Dihedral (5.8) Jugs and jams up a big dihedral to a 2-bolt anchor. **Rack:** Medium cams.

8. Lemons, Limes, and Tangerines (5.8) Climb a buttress edge past a roof (5.8). Finish above the top roof. 4 bolts to 2-bolt anchor.

9. Protection from the Virus (5.10c) Climb over the left side of a roof. Finish with a thin face. 4 bolts to 2-bolt anchor.

10. Interface (5.8) No topo. A short face route on a clean panel. Scramble

Brown Cloud Crags

onto a ledge, then balance up the face. 2 bolts to 2-bolt anchor.

11. Tenacious (5.9+) Climb past a bolt to a ledge. Continue up a pillar. 4 bolts to 2-bolt anchor.

12. Volobee (5.11b/c) 4 bolts to 2-bolt anchor.

13. Bullet the Brown Cloud (5.11a) Interesting arête. Climb to a ledge and clip a bolt. Climb the arête, then cruise to anchors. 4 bolts to 2-bolt anchor.

14. Killian's Dead (5.6) Hand crack on the right side of a panel. **Rack:** Gear to 3 inches.

15. Deck Chairs on the Titanic (5.9+) Fun and popular. A dyno crux gets you to a bolt; avoid it by jamming a crack. 6 bolts to 2-bolt anchor.

16. Windy Days (5.8) Climb to a ledge, then continue up left. 3 bolts to 2-bolt anchor.

17. Pee on D (5.8) Climb up right to a roof with anchors above. 3 bolts to 2-bolt anchor.

18. Brown Cloud Arête (5.10b) Start up an arête, then climb the right side of a pillar. 4 bolts to 2-bolt anchor.

Brown Cloud Crags

THE OVERHANG AREA

This south-facing cliff section, starting left of *Brown Cloud Arête,* is popular with lots of fun routes. The first routes start near where the access trail reaches the cliff.

Descent: Lower or rappel off fixed anchors on all routes.

19. Wholy Holy (5.8) Pull over a roof, then climb a thin pillar. 6 bolts to 2-bolt anchor.

20. Pack o' Bobs (5.7) Begins right of the access trail. Reach over a bulge, then climb a narrow panel. 4 bolts to 2-bolt anchor.

After climbing at Golden Cliffs, visit the Bradford Washburn American Mountaineering Museum at the American Mountaineering Center below the cliffs. It's the only U.S. museum dedicated to the vertical life. Find out more at www .mountaineeringmuseum.org.

21. Another Unnamed Billy Bob Route (aka Sloping Forehead) (5.7+) Companion route to *Pack o' Bobs.* A short line up the left side of an arête to a ledge with anchors. 4 bolts to 2-bolt anchor.

Overhang Area

Overhang Area

22. The Fabulous Flying Carr's Route (5.11a) Climb along a crack system to a small roof on the right side of the pillar. Step left and balance up sloping holds to the top. 5 bolts to 2-bolt anchor.

23. This Ain't Naturita, Pilgrim (5.9) Ken Trout classic. Begins where the access trail meets the cliff. Climb the left side of a pillar, keeping right of a roof. Finish with small edges up a vertical face. 5 bolts to 2-bolt anchor.

24. Smear Me a Beer (5.11b) Start 15 feet left of *Naturita*. Climb a blunt arête (crux) to its top. Step right and finish on a nice face. 7 bolts to 2-bolt anchor.

25. Hare (5.12a) Climb a seam/crack just left of a wide crack to high anchors. Stem over to the crack to ease the grade. 8 bolts to 2-bolt anchor.

26. Mrs. Hen Places a Peck (5.12a) An excellent pumpy route up a steep, clean face. 6 bolts to 2-bolt anchor.

27. Mr. Peery, Take a Bow (5.11b)
Named for Mayfield Peery, who
donated Table Mountain to climbers.
Climb past *Mrs. Hen's* first two bolts.
Where that route heads up right,
climb a slot and a rounded arête. 7
bolts to 2-bolt anchor.

28. Here Today, Gone Tomorrow
(5.9) Start below a left-facing corner
system. Climb up the corner, keeping
right of some high roofs. A right-hand
start is 5.11d. 6 bolts to 2-bolt anchor.

**29. Mr. Coors Contributes to the
Pink Stain** (5.9+) Climb past a bulge
then up a thin pillar to a final steep
face. 7 bolts to 2-bolt anchor.

30. Handle This Hard On (5.12a)
Climb up right and crank the technical crux above the first bolt. Continue
up the arête with more 5.11 cruxes
to cliff-top anchors. 5 bolts to 2-bolt
anchor.

31. Tora, Tora, Tora (5.11b/c) Climb
a crack (5.8) to a small roof to a
ledge. Finish with technical moves
to anchors. 3 bolts to 2-bolt anchor.
Rack: Stoppers and small cams.

Watch out for rattlesnakes when
you climb at the Golden Cliffs
during the warmer months.
They're often seen basking
beside the trail up to the cliff
or hiding in bushes and under
boulders on the cliff-base trail.
Keep an eye on your dog too.
Snakebites are not fun!

32. Mr. Squirrel Places a Nut (5.11c)
Classic. Face climb over a couple roofs
to a big roof. Pull over and finish up a
prow. 5 bolts to 2-bolt anchor.

33. Off Line (5.8) Climb a blunt prow
right of a deep crack. 4 bolts to 2-bolt
anchor.

34. Corniche (5.8) Jam a flared crack.
Rack: Cams to 4 inches.

35. In Between the Lines (5.9-) Face
climb through an interesting bulge
between two cracks. 5 bolts to 2-bolt
anchor.

36. Sidelines (5.10a) Climb a thin
crack, then work up left to anchors. 5
bolts to 2-bolt anchor.

Overhang Area

37. Beer Drinkers and Hell Raisers
(5.8+) Usually toproped. A thin crack climb that crosses *Sidelines*. **Rack:** Cams to 4 inches.

38. Beer Barrel Buttress (5.10c)
Climb onto a pedestal and work up the face above. 5 bolts to 2-bolt anchor.

39. The Ground Doesn't Lie
(5.10c/d) Climb steep rock to a tricky crux. 3 bolts to 2-bolt anchor.

TABLE TOP AREA
The Table Top Area is a long cliff section that ends at a gully.

Descent: Lower or rappel off fixed anchors on all routes.

40. Pigeon Pile Pinnacle (5.10d)
Hard moves over a bulge, then up the face. 5 bolts to 2-bolt anchor.

41. Lying on the Ground (5.11d) A
short, steep route on the outside of a pillar. 3 bolts to 2-bolt anchor.

42. D's Dry Dream (5.10a) Climb a
corner to a hard move onto a face. 7 bolts to 2-bolt anchor.

Table Top Area

43. Hate Hate (5.10) Reach past a bulge, then work up left to anchors.

44. Hug the Butt (5.11b) Climb an overhang to cracks and face. 5 bolts to 2-bolt anchor.

45. Death of Innocents (5.11d) Pull a tricky bulge, then climb an arête and face. 5 bolts to 2-bolt anchor.

46. Henry Spies the Line (5.10a) Face climb to a crack, then work up left along the crack. Finish with committing moves. 5 bolts to 2-bolt anchor.

47. Kevin Spies the Line (5.7+) Fun climb. Work up a slab, then grab jugs up a panel. 5 bolts to 2-bolt anchor.

48. Table Top (5.10b) Climb up right or climb direct. Continue up an arête. 4 bolts to 2-bolt anchor. **Rack:** Small to medium cams.

49. Mind Mantle Arête (5.11b) No topo. Climb up left to an arête, then climb directly up it (5.11b). 5 bolts to 2-bolt anchor.

Daniel Woods bouldering in Clear Creek Canyon.
PHOTO KEITH LADZINSKI

7.

Clear Creek Canyon

Clear Creek Canyon, a slicing gorge in the mountains west of Golden and Denver, is a sport climber's paradise. Hundreds of bolt-protected routes, ranging in difficulty from 5.4 to 5.14, are found on over forty cliffs that line the steep sides of the canyon. The cliffs, composed of 1.7-billion-year-old gneiss and schist, are climber-friendly with incut edges and crimps, sharp buckets and jugs, delicate slabs, vertical faces, and lots of over-hanging stone.

All of Clear Creek Canyon's crags are easily accessible from US 6, the main route from Denver to the gambling halls at Central City. Pullouts

near the cliffs are found along the highway. Most hiking approaches take five to ten minutes. Just be cautious and alert if you have to cross the highway or walk alongside it to access the cliffs since traffic can be heavy.

Other dangers here are loose rock and rattlesnakes. Be extremely careful not to knock any rock off since it can not only hit your belayer below but can also tumble onto the highway and cause an accident. Be alert from May through October for rattlesnakes. Lots of them live here. They're commonly found on trails and along cliff bases.

While Clear Creek Canyon is a four-season climbing area, the best

Clear Creek Canyon

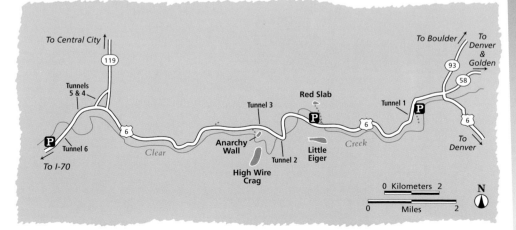

Clear Creek Canyon is one of Colorado's most recently developed climbing areas. While Layton Kor and Bob Culp did the canyon's first recorded ascent in 1961, it wasn't until 1989 that Alan Nelson, Kurt Smith, Guy Lords, and Ken Trout got out their Bosch drills and began establishing sport climbs.

climbing weather is found in spring and autumn. Expect generally mild weather with highs between 45 and 75 degrees, light precipitation, and some wind, especially in spring. Winter days can be fine for climbing if your chosen cliff is in the sun. Snowfall is usually light and melts quickly. Summer days are often hot although shaded cliffs are easily found. Little Eiger is perfect in summer, while High Wire Crag gets evening shadow.

Getting there: The cliffs at Clear Creek Canyon are easily accessed from US 6 west of Golden. To reach Golden from Denver and Denver International Airport, drive west on I-70 toward the mountains. On the west side of Denver, exit onto CO 58 at Exit 265 or US 6/Sixth Avenue at Exit 261. Drive west on either highway to their junction at the canyon mouth on the west side of Golden. To reach Golden from Boulder, drive south on CO 93 to its junction with US 6 and CO 58 at the canyon mouth.

Whether coming from Denver or Boulder, once you reach US 6, head west to drive to the cliffs. Mileages to the cliffs begin from the highway junction.

RED SLAB

The 80-foot-high Red Slab, opposite the highway and parking lot above Clear Creek, is a compact south-facing cliff with lots of good face routes. Weekends can be crowded. Most of the routes are protected by bolts. Watch for rattlesnakes in summer.

Finding the crag: Drive west from Golden on US 6 for 4.1 miles. Park in a pullout on the north side of the highway past a bridge and opposite the cliff. Cross the bridge and follow a short trail to the crag. Hiking time is five minutes.

Descent: Lower or rappel off bolt anchors on all routes.

1. Rattle and Scream (5.10a). Sustained crimps to anchors. 5 bolts to 2-bolt anchor.

2. Snakes for Snacks (5.10a) Edges and smears lead up left. 4 bolts to 2 bolt anchors.

The Red Slab was the first cliff developed in Clear Creek Canyon. In 1989 the late Alan Nelson and Kurt Smith began bolting its sport routes in a ground-up style.

Red Slab

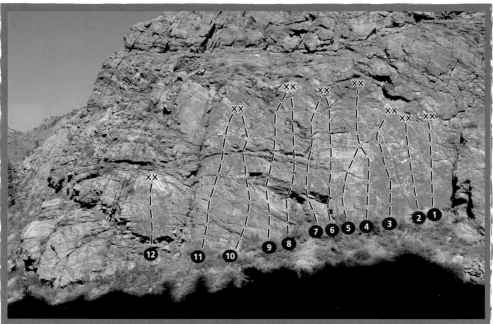

3. Lounge Lizard (5.10b/c) Climb to a thin crux above bolt 3 and finish with easier rock. 8 bolts to 2-bolt anchor.

4. Slip and Slide (5.10d). Sustained moves lead to a couple horizontal cracks. Finish direct to anchors. 7 bolts to 2-bolt anchor.

5. Pink Slip (5.12b) Hard crimpy moves, then up right above a crack. Finish up *Slip and Slide*. 8 bolts to 2-bolt anchor.

6. Diamondback (5.10c) Excellent. Begin on the right side of a roof. Climb over the roof, then face climb to a bulge. 7 bolts to 2-bolt anchor.

7. Spring Fever (5.10c) Crux moves over a roof to a seam. Finish up a headwall. 6 bolts to 2-bolt anchor.

8. Wicked Game (5.10d) A slab to a crack over a roof. Climb the roof to a thin crux. Finish up tricky rock. 6 bolts to 2-bolt anchor.

9. Trundelero (5.10b) Edge up a slab, pull over a roof, and climb to *Wicked Game*'s anchors. 8 bolts to 2-bolt anchor.

10. Vapor Trail (5.9) Climb to a roof's left edge. Move up left to anchors. 6 bolts to 2-bolt anchor.

11. Bumblies for Breakfast (5.10a) Moderate moves to a sloping crux up high. 6 bolts to 2-bolt anchor.

12. Slip It In (5.11b) Pull a roof and climb to a crux above the last bolt. 4 bolts to 2-bolt anchor.

LITTLE EIGER

Little Eiger towers above US 6 opposite Red Slab. The shady north-facing cliff, over 500 feet high from base to summit, offers lots of long, single-pitch sport routes as well as a bolted four-pitch line. Most of the routes are worthy, well protected, and cool in summer. Some anchors have open cold shuts. Use extreme caution if toproping from them; it's a good idea to clip into a lower bolt for safety. Use double ropes or a 70-meter rope on the long routes on the right side of the face. Some of the routes have dog tags, crimped on the first hanger, with the route's name, grade, and length of rope needed.

Finding the crag: Drive up US 6 for 4.1 miles (3.1 miles west of Tunnel 1). Just past a bridge over Clear Creek, park in a pull-off on the right (north) side of the highway (same parking as Red Slab). Alternatively, a larger pull-off is just east of the bridge. The cliff is obvious to the south. Cross the highway—crux of the approach—and hike up a short trail to the cliff base. Hiking approach is less than five minutes.

Descent: Lower or rappel off bolt anchors on all routes.

1. Bonehead (5.10c) Start right of a cave. Climb a thin face to a couple high cruxes. 8 bolts to 2-bolt anchor.

2. Conehead (5.11b) Grab thin holds up vertical rock. 6 bolts to 2-bolt anchor.

3. Headline (5.10a) Bouldery moves off the ground lead to a left-angling crack. Work up the crack to some laybacks. 6 bolts to 2-bolt anchor.

4. Trouthead (5.10c/d) Climb up right to a bulge to a technical crux. Finish up easier rock. 7 bolts to 2-bolt anchor.

5. Eiger Sanction (5.10d) Climb a crack to steeper rock. Work through a short crux above the fifth bolt to a sloping finish. 7 bolts to 2-bolt anchor.

6. Eiffel Tower (5.10d) Face climb to a small roof. Work over it, then climb up right along a ramp to the crux. 7 bolts to 2-bolt anchor.

7. Herbal Essence (5.10a) Climb a slab and then face moves up a black streak. 12 bolts to 2-bolt anchor.

8. Footloose (5.10a) Fun climbing. Begins right of a blank section. Climb a slab and then a steeper wall to a small roof. Finish up sloping rock. 11 bolts to 2-bolt anchor.

Little Eiger

9. First Impressions (5.9+) Great moderate. Climb left of a streak, then up the left side of a left-facing corner to tricky exit moves. 10 bolts to 2-bolt chain anchor.

10. Eiger Direct (5.11d) Excellent. Climb a slabby face to a left-facing corner topped by a roof. Pull past the roof on buckets. 10 bolts to 2-bolt anchor.

11. Radometer in the Red Zone (5.11b) Climb to a steep headwall, then pull crimps and layaways to the anchor. 6 bolts to 2-bolt anchor.

12. Too! (II 5.12a) Don't knock any rocks off! **Pitch 1:** Face climb to a crux, pass a roof, and belay at anchors. 6 bolts to 2-bolt anchor. **Pitch 2:** Work up low-angle rock to a short crux (5.5) and belay below a headwall. 1 bolt to 2-bolt anchor. **Pitch 3:** Best pitch. Grab edges up the steep headwall (5.11c) to anchors on a ledge. 10 bolts to 2-bolt anchor. **Pitch 4:** Climb past a piton and follow bolts up the steep face. Expect sustained moves (5.12a), which can be aided. 10 bolts to 2-bolt anchor. **Descent:** Make three double-rope rappels down the route. Don't dislodge rocks when pulling ropes. **Rack:** Stoppers, TCUs, and cams for pitch 2; fifteen quickdraws; two ropes; helmets.

Little Eiger

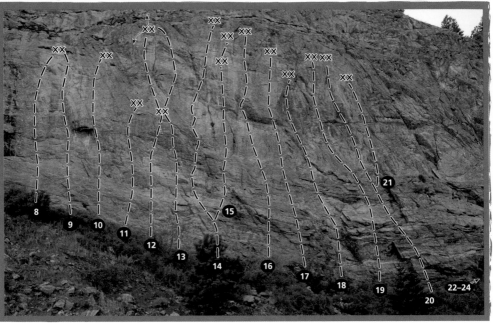

13. The Nordwand (5.11b) Great first pitch. **Pitch 1:** Climb a slab to a bulge (5.10c). 6 bolts to 2-bolt anchor. **Pitch 2:** Climb a crux bulge (5.11b/c). 6 bolts to 2-bolt anchor. **Descent:** Rappel 105 feet from the top anchors or make two rappels.

14. Natural Selection (5.11a/b) Climb a slab (5.8) to steeper rock (5.11a). 14 bolts to 2-bolt anchor. 150 feet. **Descent:** Rappel with two ropes.

15. Tierra del Fuego (5.11b) Climb a slab, then make sustained moves (5.11a) to easier climbing. Finish with more hard climbing (5.11b). 11 bolts to 2-bolt anchor. A 15-foot extension above the anchors is 5.12a.

16. Bush Administration (5.10c) Superb and interesting. Climb a slab to a steeper face with an upper bulge. 12 bolts to 2-bolt anchor. 110 feet. **Descent:** Three options—double-rope rappel, 70-meter rope, or 200-foot (60-meter) rope with a downclimb.

17. Busch Gardens (5.10b) Excellent. Belay on a ledge at the base. Climb a slab (5.9) to a pumpy roof. Finish up a headwall. 11 bolts to 2-bolt anchor. 105 feet. A 200-foot (60 meter) rope is okay.

18. The Naked Hedge (5.10b) Climb left of a left-facing corner then up broken rock. Work past an old piton to a headwall. Finish up steep rock to an arête. 13 bolts to 2-bolt anchor. 100 feet.

19. The Green Zone (5.11a) Excellent. Use a 70-meter rope. Power over an overhang (5.10c) and climb up a short left-facing corner to an overhanging crux (5.11a). Finish up easier rock (5.9+). 16 bolts to 2-bolt anchor. 120 feet.

20. Persistent Vegetative State (5.10b) Fun climbing. Use a 70-meter rope. Climb an arête right of a wave overhang and continue to a corner. Sustained climbing up the left-angling corner leads to exit moves to anchors. 15 bolts to 2-bolt anchor. 120 feet. **Descent:** Rappel with two ropes or lower with a 70-meter rope.

21. Free Up the Weed (5.11a) Start on *Persistent Vegetative State* and climb to bolt 5. Instead of climbing the corner, move straight up to the anchor with sustained climbing to a face crux right of an arête. 13 bolts to 2-bolt anchor. 90 feet.

22. The Decider (5.10a/b) No topo. Climb a steep face to a rest stance. Finish with crimps to a small roof. 11 bolts to 2-bolt anchor. 100 feet.

23. Misunderestimate (5.10b/c) No topo. Climb over a roof to easier terrain. Stem a steep corner to a move left. Continue up a technical face to a left-facing corner. 11 bolts

to 2-bolt anchor. 105 feet. **Descent:** Rappel or lower.

24. Tsunami of Charisma (5.11a/b) No topo. Use a 70-meter rope. Pull over a big roof (5.11a) to easier climbing to an overhang. Friction up a slab to a headwall and anchors. 16 bolts to 2-bolt anchor. 120 feet.

HIGH WIRE CRAG

High Wire Crag, perched up left of Tunnel 2 and US 6, is a great east-facing cliff that is stacked with moderate sport routes. It is Clear Creek Canyon's most popular cliff, so weekends can be very busy. Come early or prepare to wait in line. Beginning sport leaders like to come here too, but need to use caution as several serious accidents have occurred. Many of the routes are long, requiring either a 70-meter rope or double ropes to get back down.

High Wire Crag is best climbed in spring and autumn. Summer days can be hot but the cliff moves into the shade in later afternoon and evening, making it a pleasant destination. Winters can be cold because little sun reaches the cliff.

Finding the crag: High Wire Crag, on the east side of Tunnel 2, has a short approach along US 6. Drive west from Golden on US 6 for 6.1 miles and park at a pull-off on the right (north) side of the highway before the tunnel. Cautiously cross the highway and walk along the

High Wire Crag Overview

narrow shoulder on the highway bridge toward the tunnel. Scramble up a short, steep trail (3rd class) to the cliff base. Do not knock any rocks onto the highway! Also, do not park in the small pull-off on the south side of the highway. You will be ticketed. A large rockfall here in 2006 squashed a climber's car. The first route is where the trail meets the cliff.

> Watch where you park in Clear Creek Canyon! In 2006 a climber's car, parked just down the road from High Wire Crag, was flattened by a huge boulder that fell from the cliff above.

Descent: Lower or rappel off bolt anchors on all routes.

1. Nickels and Dimes (5.8) Short and fun. Climb up and left of a hanging flake roof. 7 bolts to 2-bolt anchor.

2. People's Choice (5.10b) Link pitches 1 and 2 or all into a single pitch. **Pitch 1:** Layback up a left-facing flake to a slab (5.10b) to a ramp. 6 bolts to 2-bolt anchor. 50 feet. **Pitch 2:** Climb featured rock (5.7) to a belay below a dihedral. 6 bolts to 2-bolt anchor. 50 feet. **Pitch 3:** Stem the overhanging dihedral to a trick exit (5.9+) and final slab. 8 bolts to 2-bolt anchor. 70 feet. **Descent:** Rappel 170 feet.

3. Slot Machine (5.11c) Climb the first two pitches of *People's Choice*. Muscle up the steep face to a wild mantle, then easier climbing. 8 bolts to 2-bolt anchor.

4. Wild Card (5.12a) Climb *People's Choice* to its second belay, then move right to another set of anchors. Use a long sling on the first bolt. Power up the steep and pumpy face. 9 bolts to 2-bolt anchor.

5. Road Kill (5.11c/d) Great route. Climb a slab with three bolts to right-angling Queen City Slab Ledge. Scramble up right to a 2-bolt belay anchor. Or just scramble up the ledge from the right to the anchor. Climb directly to a mantle to a rest stance above a roof. Continue over the big roof on jugs. Finish by going over another bulge or heading right (easier). 10 bolts to 2-bolt anchor.

6. Road Warrior (5.12c/d) Scramble up right on a ledge system to a 2-bolt belay anchor. Climb an easy slab to a corner below the big roof. Snag a rest, then motor over the roof with multiple 5.12 cruxes on great stone. 10 bolts to 2-bolt anchor.

7. Road Rash Roof (5.12a) Start right of a groove. Climb a runout slab to a big roof—heel hooks, crimps, and jams get you to the crux lip move. Finish with steep but easier stone. 11 bolts to 2-bolt anchor.

8. Jackpot (5.11d) Route ascends a dark groove. Climb the groove to devious overhanging stone. Pull through on good holds to tricky moves up high. 14 bolts to 2-bolt anchor.

9. Via Comatose Amigo (5.10b) Climb up right on slabby rock to a ledge. Move through a pegmatite band, then wander up to anchors. 13 bolts to 2-bolt anchor. **Descent:** Rappel with double ropes.

10. Dueces Wild (5.10a) Excellent! Pitches can be combined. **Pitch 1:** The route crux is the start. Hard moves to the second bolt, then jugs around the left side of a roof. Finish with a crack. 7 bolts to 2-bolt anchor. 60 feet. **Pitch 2:** Work up a slabby wall with great holds to a short headwall (5.9+) at the top. 10 bolts to 2-bolt anchor. 80 feet.

11. Passing Lane (5.9 R) Crank good holds up a face to a dicey runout traverse left. Exit onto the slabby wall above and cruise to anchors. 7 bolts to 2-bolt anchor.

12. Overpass (5.11c) A powerful start with a mantle, tricky second clip, and arête leads to a fun slab finish. 8 bolts to 2-bolt anchor.

13. Crackerjack (5.8+) On the left side of the buttress. Jam a steep crack over a bulge to a seam. Finish up right with fun slabbing to anchors. 8 bolts to 2-bolt anchor.

High Wire Crag—Left

14. Ace in the Hold (5.10-) Clamber up a gully, then step left onto a prow. Work up the face to a crux above bolt 5. 9 bolts to 2-bolt anchor.

15. Fifth of July (5.9) Fantastic climbing! A hard start leads to fine face climbing. 10 bolts to 2-bolt anchor. 90 feet.

16. Stone Cold Moderate (5.7) Popular, fun, and easy. Start at the left side of an alcove. A tough start with big holds pulls a bulge. Cruise the dihedral above to a ledge with anchors. 7 bolts to 2-bolt anchor.

17. Poker Face (5.8+) A boulder problem start with a crucial pocket leads to fun slabby rock. 8 bolts to 2-bolt anchor.

18. Pony Up (5.8) Left companion to *Poker Face*. Work up the tricky start to easier rock. 7 bolts to 2-bolt anchor.

ANARCHY WALL

The west-facing Anarchy Wall, one of Clear Creek's best cliffs, has excellent 5.12s on its steep face. A variety of moves give maximum pump value. This is a hardman's cliff, with only a couple easier warm-ups.

The wall is best during cooler temperatures in spring and autumn. In summer, plan on coming in the morning to climb in the shade to avoid greasing off slick holds.

Chuck Fryburger sees the light on the *Anarchitect* (5.12d) on the Anarchy Wall. PHOTO KEITH LADZINSKI

Finding the crag: Drive up the canyon and park at 6.4 miles on the south side of US 6 just past Tunnel 2. It's best to approach this parking lot from the eastbound lane. Because of heavy traffic, westbound drivers may find it difficult to make the left turn into the parking area, in which case it's better to drive farther up the road until you can turn around. Scramble to the rock base. Approach time from car to cliff is under five minutes.

Descent: Lower or rappel off bolt anchors on all routes.

1. Question Authority (5.12a) Fun route on the right side. 3 bolts to 2-bolt anchor.

2. Chaos (5.13a) Bouldery route with a crux at the first bolt. It's best to stick-clip the first two bolts and use a single carabiner on bolt 2. The first moves are 5.13 crimps, and the ledge below is an ankle-buster. 4 bolts to 2-bolt anchor.

3. Crackpot (5.12c) Grand traverse. Jam a crack (5.11) up left across *Anarchitect* and continue left along the crack to an alcove rest on *Presto*. Finish up *Presto*. 10 bolts to 2-bolt anchor.

4. Anarchitect (5.12d) Classic route up the 110-degree overhanging wall. Climb steep rock and work up balancy crux moves to a deadpoint. Save

Anarchy Wall

something for the pumpy redpoint crux. 7 bolts to 2-bolt anchor.

5. Maestro (5.12d) Excellent and thuggish. Hard moves (5.12a) lead to a shake-out alcove rest. Climb up right until you can't move, then throw a jam in a slot. Finish up right. 6 bolts to 2-bolt anchor.

6. Presto (5.12c) Hard and pumpy, but has three rests. Start up *Maestro* (5.12a) but move up left above bolt 4. Climb to a rest at a slot. Crimp thin moves (5.12a), then step around a corner for the last rest. End with the technical crux (5.12b) on a final face. 8 bolts to 2-bolt anchor.

7. Matriarch (5.12d) Direct start to *Presto*. Hard moves to a sloping shelf, then up to a right-facing arch and a crux dyno to slopers. Continue past *Presto*'s second rest and finish to anchors. 7 bolts to 2-bolt anchor.

8. Monkey Wrench (5.11c) Short, steep, and sweet with sloper holds that angle the wrong way. 4 bolts to 2-bolt anchor.

9. Anarchy Rules (5.12b) Power moves. Climb sustained crimps and slopers to the *Monkey Wrench* anchors. 5 bolts to 2-bolt anchor.

10. Anarchy in the UK (5.12b) Fine technical power moves. Climb tricky rock to anchors above a steep section. 3 bolts to 2-bolt anchor.

11. Power Trip (5.12a) A basic jug haul with a kneebar at the crux and hard final moves. 5 bolts to 2-bolt anchor.

12. Hazardous Waste (5.11d) The usual warm-up. Climb a blocky edge to a small roof. Finish with crimps or a long reach. 4 bolts to 2-bolt anchor.

13. Anatomic (5.12c) A traverse that includes the cruxes of four routes. Begin at *Monkey Wrench*'s first bolt. Climb up left, first crimpy and thin and then powerful and pumpy, to the chain anchors on *Hazardous Waste*. 9 bolts to 2-bolt anchor.

Appendix: Climbing Shops, Gyms, Guide Services, and Hospitals

Climbing Shops and Gyms

Basecamp Mountain Sports
821 Pearl St.
Boulder, CO 80302
(303) 443-6770

Bent Gate Mountaineering
1300 Washington Ave.
Golden, CO 80401
(303) 271-9382 or (877) BENT-GATE
www.bentgate.com

Boulder Mountaineer
1335 Broadway
Boulder, CO 80302
(303) 442-8355

Boulder Rock Club
2952 Baseline Rd.
Boulder, CO 80303
(303) 447-2804

Lowe Alpine Retail Store
2325 W. Midway Blvd.
Broomfield, CO 80020
(303) 465-2072

Mountain Sports
821 Pearl St.
Boulder, CO 80302
(303) 443-6770

Neptune Mountaineering
633 S. Broadway, Suite A
Boulder, CO 80305
(303) 499-8866
www.neptunemountaineering.com

The North Face
629-K S. Broadway
Boulder, CO 80303
(303) 499-1731
www.thenorthface.com

REI
1789 28th St.
Boulder, CO 80301
(303) 583-9970

REI
1416 Platte St.
Denver, CO 80202
(303) 756-3100

REI
9637 E. County Line Rd.
Englewood, CO 80112
(303) 858-1726

REI
5375 S. Wadsworth Blvd.
Lakewood, CO 80123
(303) 932-0600

Wilderness Exchange
2401 15th St., Suite 90
Denver CO 80202
(303) 964-0708
www.wildernessexchangeunlimited
.com

Guide Services
Bob Culp Climbing School
1201 Mountain Pines Rd.
Boulder, CO 80302
(303) 444-0940
www.bobculp.com

**Colorado Mountain School/Boulder
Rock Club**
2829 Mapleton Ave.
Boulder CO 80301
(800) 836-4008
www.totalclimbing.com

Front Range Climbing Company
1370 Windmill Ave.
Colorado Springs, CO 80907
(866) 572-3722
www.frontrangeclimbing.com

Hospitals
Boulder Community Hospital
P.O. Box 9019
1100 Balsam (North Broadway and
Balsam)
Boulder, CO 80301-9019
(303) 440-2273
www.bch.org

**Denver Presbyterian St. Luke's
Medical Center**
1719 E. 19th Ave.
Denver, CO
(303) 839-6000
www.pslmc.com

St. Anthony Central Hospital
4231 W. 16th Ave.
Denver, CO 80204
(303) 629-3511
www.stanthonycentral.org

University of Colorado Hospital
4200 E. 9th Ave.
Denver, CO 80262
(303) 372-0000
www.uch.edu

Index

About the Author

Stewart M. Green, living in Colorado Springs, Colorado, is a contract writer and photographer for FalconGuides/Globe Pequot Press. He's written over 20 travel and climbing books for Globe Pequot, including *KNACK Rock Climbing, Rock Climbing Colorado, Rock Climbing Europe, Rock Climbing Utah, Rock Climbing Arizona,* and *Rock Climbing New England.* Stewart, a life-long climber, began his climbing career in Colorado at age twelve and has since climbed all over the world. He's also a professional climbing guide with Front Range Climbing Company and the About.com Guide to Climbing. Visit him at www.stewartgreen.com.

PROTECTING CLIMBING ACCESS SINCE 1991